Mount Mills
(Woollen)

44" .439

School

Mount House 24 2·054

Almshouses 27 .298

Cattle Pens

STA

26 ·644

B.M.278·9

28 St.Mary's Church 1·488

Grave Yard

GREEN 275

277 Police Station

Church House

272

Rectory 29 2·985 *St.Mary's* (Rectory)

F.P.

38 2·116

30 3·547

B.M.284·5

274

283

Grammar School

31

33 9+3

F.P.

ROUND THE SQUARE IN WITNEY

FRONT COVER: The author, keeping an eye on the Square 1911
(WTR), and a Church Schools procession marching through the Square,
1907. (PR)

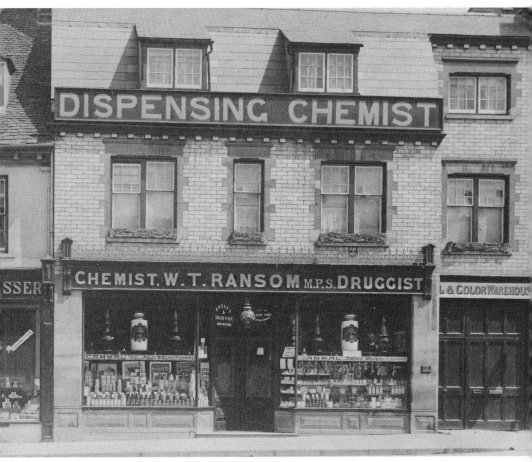

The chemist's shop, about 1904; before deciding to let the lefthand side, Father used it as an office, but kept the window dressed. (WTR)

ROUND
THE SQUARE
IN WITNEY

BY

PHYLLIS RANSOM

All good wishes
Phyllis Ransom.

BARRACUDA BOOKS LIMITED
BUCKINGHAM, ENGLAND
MCMLXXXVIII

PUBLISHED BY BARRACUDA BOOKS LIMITED
BUCKINGHAM, ENGLAND
AND PRINTED BY
THE DEVONSHIRE PRESS LIMITED
TORQUAY, ENGLAND

BOUND BY
J. W. BRAITHWAITE & SONS LIMITED
WOLVERHAMPTON, ENGLAND

JACKET PRINTED BY
CHENEY & SONS LIMITED
BANBURY, OXON

LITHOGRAPHY BY
MRM GRAPHICS LIMITED
WINSLOW, ENGLAND

TYPESET IN
10/11pt BASKERVILLE BY
KEY COMPOSITION
NORTHAMPTON, ENGLAND

ISBN 0 86023 416 9

Contents

Dedication

to the memory of
my Father, Mother and Sister and to
all who worked in the old chemist's shop

Acknowledgements

So many people have helped me in so many ways I don't know how to thank them, but this is an attempt. Jill Hoyle encouraged the writing of this book and many friends jogged my memory. I already had a number of illustrations; many of them are family snaps taken by my father, W. T. Ransom, or ones I found lying about in the places where such things do lie when a family has lived in the same house for fifty-four years. The leaflets had been kept by my mother, who hated throwing anything away and endured teasing about it. Still, there were gaps, but happily no lack of kind people to fill them.

Tom Worley not only let me take everything I wanted from his extensive collection of old photographs but provided dates and other information from his researches into Witney history. Besides giving me the freedom of his case of slides, Peter Barker went to immense trouble photographing the new features of the Market Square, and June Barker had pictures to lend as well. Jean Fletcher, Joan Ford, née Cadel, Mary Ford, née Cadel, and Ian Leigh also lent photographs and answered questions, and Amy Brooks, née Barrell, let me draw on her great knowledge of the Square. I am deeply grateful to them all.

Fred Fletcher and John Fletcher told me about the church bells and carillon, and the Huddleston family — Betty Huddleston, Georgina Edwards and Barbara Hadland — supplied facts about the cinema. Vera Barnes, Jack Barnes, Phyllis Rumbelow-Pearce, née Bartlett, Frank Bishop and Joe Jones each gave me an anecdote, and Harold Turner not only read what I had written about the Fire Brigade but made me write it all over again and let me see old log books. How can one give loud enough thanks for all that?

Help of another kind came from Joan Gott, who gave guidance for the index, and Mark Campbell of Proctor's — High Street offspring of our old chemist's shop in the Market Square — who let me look round his dispensary to see how things have changed. The staff of Witney, Burford and Woodstock Libraries dealt with taking subscribers' names, the Librarian of the Local History Library in Oxford supplied the map, and the Editor of the _Witney Gazette_ allowed reproduction of a photograph which appeared in that paper in 1971. Thank you, everybody.

For me it has been a pleasant trip into nostalgia. I hope the book will raise a few smiles from all readers and a 'Yes, that's how it used to be' from my contemporaries as well.

Before my time: 1896. Mr Gerring is running a chemist's shop, but the two houses on the left have still to be turned into a toyshop and a hairdresser's. Territorials are on parade. (PR)

Key to Caption Credits

ABOVE: About 1902, the two houses have been converted, and Mr Moore has a toyshop. Mr Keen has taken over the chemist's business which my father bought from him in 1904. The schoolchildren are having a school treat. BELOW: In 1931, Mr John Welch, solicitor, now occupies the lefthand side. He opened his first office there and it was soon too small for him. The two pharmacies are very close to one another — Mr Neave's is in the detached block of buildings. (Both PR)

Round the Square

It was my good fortune to be born in the Market Square of a small town on the fringe of the Cotswolds and to live there for over half a century, convinced for years that it was the centre of the world. And why not? It was certainly the centre of the town and everybody came there, from a duke and a princess to the organ-grinder and the knife-grinder; everything took place there, from a meet of the Old Berks to a military parade, from the sale of cabbages to the proclamation of kings.

All this was displayed, not only where I could see it, but see it well. We lived upstairs, over our chemist's shop, and there was nothing to get in the way. The trees were on the other side of the Square and the small lamp-post was in the middle, shedding a soft and soothing light instead of the evil-coloured glare which is the gift of progress.

That lamp-post was a joy. A lamp-lighter on a bicycle used to make me think of knights in armour when, without dismounting, he tilted at the lamp with a long pole like a lance and never seemed to miss. It shed its light on so much that was interesting and beautiful, especially on Christmas Eve, when a choir formed a circle round it and sang Christmas carols. As I listened, lying in my warm bed or peeping out of the window, the singing always mingled with the expectation of presents, plum pudding and fun, and was like a foretaste of heaven.

There were other comfortable sounds which I could hear all the year round, and at night they made me feel safe. The church clock sounded the quarters and numbered the hours, though I could not always be sure what hour it was. The Buttercross clock struck at the same time but not at the same speed, so it was only in the small hours that I could disentangle the two sounds. This problem was not solved until about 1960, when the ship's bell which had provided the Buttercross clock with a voice was silenced, and St Mary's had the air to itself.

The church carillon played a tune at every third hour, day and night. From its wide repertory I remember best how it asked gentle Jesus, meek and mild, to look upon a little child, called upon us to count our blessings, assured us there was no place like home, bade farewell to the last rose of summer, and announced that our Highland Laddie had gone with streaming banners where noble deeds were done. Like the church bells, the carillon was silenced during Hitler's War. Fewer tunes are played now, some favourites of mine have gone, and some of the hymns which are left ring out a little jerkily when notes are missing. I should love to hear the silenced ones again, and to hear them during the night, when the carillon is now quiet out of respect for the people it used to disturb.

Many years ago it was proposed that the Square should have a clock tower of its own, but it was decided that the best place for a clock was the church tower. This meant a daily climb for a man who kept it going. The last of these was Mr Fletcher who told me that after toiling up the spiral staircase every day for over twenty-one years, he decided that enough was enough, was replaced by electricity, and liked to recall that he had been paid ten shillings a week.

The whole Market Square is divided into three sections by two blocks of buildings, like two islands in a lake. From my favourite window I watched over the central part and, only by leaning out, could I see where the Square merged with the beautiful Church Green to my left and narrowed into High Street on my right.

To my far left, on the opposite side, a former seed merchant's shop is now part of an electricity showroom, so no longer can you buy there the kind of seed which sprang into colour in our garden, or the kind the canary ate. I used to run across to buy bran for the rabbits, biscuits for the dogs, and corn for Mother's disagreeable hens, which she cherished long after they had forgotten all about laying eggs.

Next to this was Mr Tarrant's grocery, which is about to be swallowed up by Barclay's Bank. I have seen this building change its appearance several times, but never more spectacularly than on the evening of the day when George V was crowned, in June, 1911.

That afternoon a procession, headed by the Town Band, had walked through the Square with me in it, waving a Union Jack and coveting the wreaths of flowers held aloft on poles by the lines of schoolchildren just in front. I was wearing a white dress and a white bonnet with rosettes over the ears and a big bow under the chin. Resisting all the attempts kind grown-ups made to carry me, I plodded along the town's mile-long processional way, starting on the Green by Holy Trinity Church at one end, and finishing in the Recreation Ground by St Mary's Church at the other. This ground is called the Leys.

That was the first time I marched along the traditional route, but I have done it many times since, and will gladly have a shot at it again

12

should there come an occasion for such jollity. The last time was towards the end of Hitler's War when I wore navy slacks, a navy greatcoat with silver buttons, and a tin hat with 'RC' for 'Report Centre' painted on the front.

When we had reached the Leys on this Coronation Day, I sat with my elder sister on a wooden bench — the sort that tips up if you sit alone on one end of it — and we were brought some tea in a bucket. We drank it from cups of delicate white china with the heads of the new King and Queen pictured on both cup and saucer, and we were allowed to take these trophies home. The cups were dipped in the bucket and I hate to think what happened if you had a second cupful.

Races and other sports were taking place but I was considered too small to compete in any of these, just as I was considered too small to stay for the bonfire and fireworks which were the climax of all this fun. While my sister stayed with the grown-ups, I was sent home with our much-loved mother's help. Mary was young, and probably as reluctant to go as I was but, before the others came back, we watched the biggest bonfire in the district on that illuminated day.

The grocer's house and shop across the Square went up in flames. It was a magnificent sight. I watched it through the bars which prevented my falling out of my top storey bedroom window, half thrilled and half afraid.

I remember dark smoke and bright flame, a horrid cracking noise and a horrible smell. People came running from all directions and got in the way of the Fire Brigade, which came galloping up the Hill from High Street. The fire engine was drawn by two horses with jingling brass bells on their harness, and the firemen were grand in navy blue uniform with brass buttons, high boots, and magnificent brass helmets which caught the light from the flames. I knew that one of these was bobbing about on my uncle's head. When it was not there, it hung with a hatchet from the ceiling of his hall, so that both could be snatched down when he was called to a fire by a breathless boy on a bicycle.

Sleep overcame me before the firemen conquered the blaze. Next day the town rang with excited chatter because it was the house of Councillor Tarrant, chosen to light the official bonfire, which had 'burst into flames at the very same minute', while I was able to boast to my sister that my bonfire had been bigger than hers.

A boy who helped carry out the damaged stock from the shop was still wondering in his eighties how the big square biscuit tins, their lids sealed and looking perfectly sound, turned out to be full of water.

Before its end as a grocery, the shop was attacked by modernisation, so that its customers had to hunt for what they wanted along the shelves, instead of having it comfortably handed to them over a counter.

Its neighbour was a bank, called Gillett's, and it is still there under the name of Barclay. One morning in 1904, when my father opened the shop door on his very first day in a business of his own, he found the manager of Gillett's Bank standing on the doorstep, waiting to ask if he would open an account. Father agreed, because he admired the manager's energy, and thought his few coins might as well rattle about in Gillett's vaults as in anybody else's. A few minutes afterwards the manager of another bank arrived on the same errand and must have been surprised to find that he was already too late.

These two banks in the Square were separated only by the Marlborough Hotel and a shop. The hotel was well worth watching, because you could see all sorts of people going in and out and, with any luck, there would be one who had drunk more than was good for him. My favourite was usually helped onto his bike and given a push to send him off down the Hill into High Street. Mother and Father could sometimes be heard wondering how he managed to balance on a bicycle when plainly he couldn't balance on his feet, but what puzzled me was how he got off at the other end. There couldn't always be somebody there waiting and ready to help him, could there? I didn't know what it felt like to be tipsy but I did know how it hurt to fall off a bicycle. There were no 'fairy cycles' in my time; children learnt to ride on quite heavy ones, just like those the grown-ups had except for their size.

The shop next to the hotel was kept by two sisters, who sold a jolly mixture of clocks, watches, jewellery and such household silver as eggspoons and butter dishes, with tobacco and cigarettes. They were devoted to animals. Every time Jo, our little Pomeranian, had puppies, we took them over to be fondled and admired, and the sisters even tried to look pleased when I showed them Jehu, Jericho and Jehosaphat, the three black mice I had trained to sit on cotton reels in imitation of lions in a circus. 'Oh, aren't they sweet?' chirped the ladies, grasping their long, dark skirts and standing as far back from the counter as they could.

Next to the second bank was a saddler's where you could sniff up and enjoy the lovely smell of leather while asking for a portmanteau to be stitched or a dog's harness made to measure, and you were never given a list of good reasons why these things could not be done. Then came a pub, mysteriously called Hun Tedmunds, a very confusing name to have when we were busy fighting the Huns in the Kaiser's War. Its proper name was, and is, the Eagle Vaults, but I had never heard it called that, and think of it under the old name still, though it no longer belongs to Messrs Hunt Edmunds. The old saddler's shop now forms part of it.

The last building I could see from my window on that side of the Square was a large private house, with a flight of stone steps leading to the front door. In it lived Dr Batt and his large family. A tablet in St Mary's Church now commemorates the five generations of that name which practised as surgeons in the town for nearly two hundred years, and the gift of this home in 1926 to church and parish for the use of children. A department of the Technical College now occupies the house and a Primary School flourishes in the grounds behind it.

At my end of the right-hand block of buildings was the Other Chemist, Mr Neave, and it was strange to see, after so many years, oranges and greens where his lovely carboys of coloured water used to stand. Another change of ownership has filled the windows with glass and china. The friendship between my father and Mr Neave confounded the old saying that two of a trade never agree, and both confused and amused the commercial travellers who visited the pair of them.

I had to lean out of the window to see the toyshop on our side, whose windows came so close to the ground that no child was too small to look in them. In later years I came to think of this shop as accident-prone. Twice I saw a car parked across the Square suddenly start moving without apparent reason and wander over to examine Mrs Cadel's window by itself. Twice I saw the shop on fire.

One Sunday afternoon in the fifties, hearing a disturbance, I looked out to find a small crowd gathering in the Square below, smoke billowing out of the toyshop's door, and the Other Chemist's partner hurrying across with the fire extinguisher. The blaze did not spread to the house, was soon put out, and was not very serious as fires go.

Soon after opening time some years later, I heard a disturbance, looked out to see a large, excited crowd gathering, smoke billowing out of the toyshop's door and, to complete the picture, the Other Chemist's partner hurrying across with a fire extinguisher. This encore could scarcely be believed, and I stood for some seconds paralysed by sheer astonishment before rushing to fetch our own Minimax. I could barely lift it, and was thankful to have it snatched away by a man who could. He returned it later with a graphic descripton of its inadequacy. By this time the Fire Brigade was busy. It was not long before Guy Fawkes Day, a bad time of year to have a fire if you stocked fireworks, and this was a very bad and noisy fire. In time a new shop was open for 'Business as Usual' but now, as another office, it's a sad loss to children.

Between the toyshop and our pharmacy was sandwiched a hair-dresser's which, in the time of Mr Burton, housed the telephone exchange as well. This also survived a fire, which never really got going, as my father rushed in with the extinguisher in time to deal with a beam smouldering in the chimney. He was delighted with his success and much amused and astonished when the insurance company, in its delight, insisted on giving him a new pair of trousers.

To complete this bright ring of flame I will for a moment skip over our house and shop to that part of the Square almost touching Church Green. There a tailor and outfitter's was burnt down one night in George V's coronation year, and the tenant saved himself by sliding down a drainpipe in his nightwear. Then he went to Australia, or perhaps it was New Zealand, and our cinema rose on the site, with the evocative name of Electric Theatre. This was later changed to People's Palace.

My sister had already seen a moving picture in a sideshow at our annual Fair and, as she had described it to me many times, I almost felt I had seen it too. After watching spangled dancing-girls kicking and swaying on a platform outside a big tent, she had bought a penny ticket to go through its ornately painted and gilded front, and stood inside for the few minutes it took to show a sample of the short action pictures in trick photography which were among the first movies ever made.

A man walking along a street was run over by a steam-roller and left lying on the ground 'as flat as a paper pattern of a man'. Then someone came along with a pump and blew air into him until he could stand up and walk away, looking as good as new. That was all, and a thrill for people who were seeing pictures move for the first time.

My first few visits to the real cinema were occasions for wonder and fear. A favourite trick of the early cameramen was making cars charge straight at the audience, and this was terrifying. Just at the moment when you felt sure the car was going to run amok among the seats, a swiftly widening gap appeared between its front wheels and it vanished, leaving the impression that it had split asunder.

I had to see this vanishing trick a number of times before I could watch it without flinching. In a very different type of film I was terrified when a beautiful girl in a torn dress was imprisoned by cannibals in a cage made of branches from a tree. She thrust her arms through the bars in a silent plea for mercy, and I had never before seen anyone with such wide-open eyes. Nor had I learnt that the hero always appeared in the nick of time. Another film which haunted me showed people hiding in a loft, where we had reason to think they were safe until a trapdoor slowly opened, a black face appeared under a white turban, and a pair of white eyeballs rolled round and round in a most sinister manner. I don't remember the outcome of all this, but no doubt there was somewhere a hero who kept to the rules.

Looking back, I think there was something in the very quality of silence which made these old films particularly terrifying, and the terror was accentuated by a pianist, who built up an eerie atmosphere round ghosts and horrors and apprehension of the unknown. She also used music to emphasise the excitement of a galloping chase and hearty fighting; it played up to slapstick and glided into dreaminess for what I called the 'lovey-dovey'. What fun it would be, I used to think as I grew more wise to the ways of the cinema, if she played lovey-dovey music while the good cowboys were chasing the bad ones, or swung into a gallop when Little Lord Fauntleroy was being kissed by Dearest, but she never did; how did Mrs Huddleston always know what was coming next?

The film which showed me that the cinema could be a place of enchantment, in spite of threatening cars and wicked cannibals, was a version of Hans Andersen's *Little Mermaid,* in which a famous swimmer, Annette Kellerman, took part. The underwater scenes with the baby mermaids, the mermaid's tail visibly splitting into the legs on which she walked so painfully, and her romantic dresses were pure magic to my sister and me.

The breathtaking serials came along when we had learned not to take things too seriously. Influenced by my sister, I could even laugh at them, though each week the heroine was left in an appalling predicament when the text flashed upon the screen urging us to return next week to see another thrilling instalment of this exciting serial. I remember seeing a heroine — probably played by Pearl White — tied to some sort of table in some sort of cave, gazing wide-eyed at an immense slab of rock suspended above her, with a sharp spike protruding from it for good measure. It was suspended by a rope which was being slowly burnt through by the flame of a candle, and there were only a few fibres left when we were invited to return next week.

As my sister and I were not allowed to go to the cinema very often, it was only once that I saw two consecutive episodes. The heroine — probably the same one — was tied to a tree beside a waterhole, and all the ferocious animals in the jungle were padding through the trees for their evening drink. There we left her. Next week the hero rushed in, slashed at her bonds with a knife, and ran away with her so easily that I thought it quite tame and didn't mind having missed all the other rescues.

By this time I'd become hardened to wide-open eyes, rolling eyeballs, cold staring eyes, roving eyes, roguish eyes, and almost every expression those over-worked features of the face were called upon to produce in the days when the voice had to be silent. The heroines spent so much time being horror-stricken, with eyes as wide open as they could be forced to go, that it is a wonder the eyelids ever came down again, but down they did come to cover happy eyes at the end, when each beautiful girl collected her kiss.

As I had seen the Picture Palace being built, I hated seeing it empty and forlorn when cinema audiences stayed at home to watch

TV and the building was closed after a flirtation with Bingo. It is now full of activity again under the general name of 'Palace' as several managements work within it to provide a club, bar, restaurant, and fitness studio offering a gymnasium, saunas and a solarium. Films are to be shown again on Saturdays, so we may once more see queues of lively children waiting to go in.

My old home suffered a worse fate, as it was bulldozed away in 1969, just over ten years after our successor had taken over the shop. My father had been another chemist's successor in 1904. When he died in 1942 my sister, who had been his partner for some years, ran the business until her own health failed in 1957, so that between them they had run it for fifty-three years. When we had to leave, we moved only a few hundred yards away.

The house and shop were taken down so that cars could enter the supermarket's carpark which was to absorb our garden and those of our neighbours. The calf which is worshipped now is made of baser stuff than gold; its temples are wastes of concrete and fumes of petrol are its incense. I can remember when a car passing through the Square was an event, that I would strain my neck trying to read its numberplate, and was really excited when I first saw one driven by a woman.

I had to see them driven over what had been the floors of the shop, the house and the warehouses, to park where the gooseberries and potatoes used to grow among the lavender and lawns. I forced myself to look when the building was almost demolished, and thought of the wry comments my father would have made if he had seen the board proclaiming that the firm tearing it to pieces was called 'The United'.

When I walked down the completed carpark to see if there could possibly remain any trace of the years my family had spent there, I found two. Still hanging from the neighbouring Corn Exchange wall was the earth wire from Father's first wireless set — the one with the earphones, which we had to share to hear the sounds coming from 2 LO — the voices of Stainless Stephen, Clapham and Dwyer, Mabel Constanduros and Big Ben. Still firmly wedged in the Corn Exchange wall, not far from the ground, was a large pebble from Sheringham beach, once the pride of my minnow aquarium which, as a child, I'd hammered into a ventilation hole, because its grating was broken and I thought rats might come in that way. I had never seen a rat and had no special reason to think they lived in the Corn Exchange, but I had heard grown-ups whispering about them. I felt sure voices would not be hushed when I was around if there were not something fearful about rats, so this seemed a reasonable precaution to take against the unknown creatures.

A piece of wire and a pebble! As I looked round the bleak open space which would soon be filled with cars — mine ruefully among

18

them — I remembered how I had first seen our part of it as a gravelled yard between the ferns and holly against the Corn Exchange wall, and the geraniums in tubs against the old stone outhouses on the other side. On some of these, even then, time had started the work of demolition. There were warehouses, and a wash-house with a copper which had blazed and bubbled every Monday. Next came a big open shed containing extraordinary junk, an empty pigsty built of great stone slabs full of fossils, and a couple of long-disused earth closets, one of them a two-seater. There were stables, where all Jo's puppies had been born, a henhouse with a long run where the rabbits lived after all the hens had died, ladders and trees to climb, and a loft to read in when it was too cold on the roof of the cart-shed. Besides taking a book, I used to climb up there with other necessities for my comfort. These were Brit, my own little Pomeranian, who was quite happy about it, a doll, and an old mineral water bottle in which tap water was imprisoned by a fascinating spring stopper.

The yard led to a high-walled garden which Mother, in spite of the dogs, rabbits and children who ran about there, kept full of flowers and fruit, and where I played games which were very much alike whether they were called Red Indians, Girl Guides, Soldiers, or Desert Islands. More often than not I played them alone. Even for the Guides they involved weapons, either homemade bows and arrows or bought pop-guns, besides walking about on stilts and foraging for food. This was a pleasant occupation as none of it was forbidden and I ate at will raw carrots and rhubarb, raspberries, gooseberries, strawberries and currants, tumbledown apples, plums and pears, and much besides without suffering any kind of qualm.

My special desert island book was Lamb's *Tales from Shakespeare*, but it was a grown-ups' magazine which influenced my garden playtime all one summer. *Home Notes* was passed on to me because it contained a picture-strip called 'Jungle Jinks'; I was mildly interested in assorted animals who dressed and behaved like schoolboys, but absolutely fascinated by the back page, where people asked very peculiar questions and had them answered by somebody's auntie. I loved, too, the short paragraphs of society gossip that were almost as puzzling, and from one of these I learnt that Queen Mary collected old china.

I took a special interest in Queen Mary because of my part in the coronation, and I thought that was a queer thing for her to do. Why did she want old china when she could afford to pay for new? Just look at all those diamond necklaces! However, what was good enough for Queen Mary was clearly good enough for me; I knew where old china was to be found and set about collecting it.

It was a peculiarity of our garden that the soil was peppered with broken bits of crockery, about the size of a postage stamp; plain, coloured, patterned, pretty, dull, coarse and fine; there was no lack of variety. The trouble was that there was no lack of china either, and by the time I'd filled a large box hidden in the greenhouse I was heartily tired of the whole affair and willing to leave the rest for Her Majesty, if she really wanted it. Anyone could tell from her photographs that Queen Mary would never do anything naughty or silly, but grubbing about in the garden of Buckingham Palace did seem a strange pastime for a lady who could wear a crown on her head.

I was not allowed to play outside in the Square, where it was chiefly boys who gathered together. In later days, when cars swept across it from four directions, or still later ones when they were parked solidly in it, it was hard to believe what a good playground the Square had been. I had no such smooth surface for spinning my tops but, out there, the boys who could whip them round with ease for ever and ever stirred my admiration and envy, especially when they caught up a pegtop in a whiplash so that it leapt into the air, landed safely, and went on spinning. There was a group of boys who would start their pegtops turning up by the Water Tower, about three quarters of a mile away, and whip them in a series of leaps down the hill, along Corn Street and round the corner into the Square, where they would still keep them going in spite of other boys dashing to and fro on roller skates or playing cricket, with a soft ball, and a rolled up jacket for stumps. In due season came other pastimes, such as bowling hoops or rolling marbles.

I don't know what Women's Lib would have had to say about the convention that girls had wooden hoops, which they struck with sticks shaped rather like drumsticks, while boys had iron ones, which they scooped along with a metal rod looking rather like a giant's button-hook. I could manage both kinds and never thought to question why my own had to be made of wood, though I did resent a similar convention that, on the seashore, boys should have metal spades and girls wooden ones, which allowed no serious digging but just a frustrated scraping that left little more than a ridged pattern in firm sand.

In winter came the glory of sliding. If really big boys came along, the slide might stretch nearly from one side of the Square to the other, and I watched long chains of children playing Follow my Leader. Usually it wasn't long before a policeman arrived to stop the fun, and a man followed to scatter gravel and kill the slide stone dead. It was explained to me that these slides were dangerous: a grown-up might step on them and have a serious fall. I thought grown-ups should have the sense to put their feet elsewhere; the Square was big enough.

Often on Sunday mornings the really big boys came along with a football and kicked it about so vigorously that shopkeepers became nervous about their plate glass windows, so this game had to be stopped too.

Besides these unofficial pastimes, other entertainments came to the Square. The earliest I can remember is Bostock and Wombwell's Menagerie. The vans the animals travelled in were arranged in a rectangle, with a gap where you paid to go in and then found that the inner sides of the vans had been taken away to reveal animals behind bars. It was all very stuffy and smelly, and there wasn't much room for either people or animals. The man who went into the lion's cage was quite rough with it and, when he forced open the poor creature's mouth and put his own head between its teeth for a long moment, it was all quite horrid. There were monkeys, which jumped about in a funny way but had sad faces. I liked the armadilloes but, on the whole, was glad to go home. We slept within a few yards of all those animals that night and I hoped they wouldn't get out, though I should have liked the lion and the monkeys to be allowed to go home too.

This must have been one of the last of such entertainments to take place in the Square, for either Church Green or the Leys came to be used as these were considered more suitable. The annual Fair had been held in the Square at one time.

Brass Bands came quite often. Some, called German Bands, would play rousing marches and happy tunes but, when the Kaiser's War started, people said they had all been spies. The Town Band would pom-pom away, and so would the Salvation Army's. The Army had people who preached and prayed and sang as well, mostly hymn tunes, and there were ladies with pretty bonnets, so they provided the most variety.

Several times — and I can't remember for what entertainment — the man who collected the money came round walking on stilts so high that he could hand us the box as we sat at our upstairs window. He wore tremendously long trousers and it was a mystery to me how he put them on. My sister and I decided we should like a pair of stilts, so Father had some made for us. I doubt if they increased our height by more than a foot and, as he insisted that they should be very strong, they were also very heavy. However, it was easy enough to balance on them and I even managed to perform some kind of dancing step which I insisted was the polka.

Another sound of music we all knew well in the old days was the barrel-organ's. I enjoyed this best when the man did not have a sad-faced little monkey chained to his instrument, but always the busy handle produced a twanging rhythm and a tingling succession of runs which none of the bands could beat.

The knife-grinder who pushed his travelling handcart into the Square would not have thought of himself as an entertainer but what fun it was to watch the sparks fly as he sat there sharpening our scissors and knives, and the men who sat on our doorstep exercising other skills were fascinating too as they re-seated cane chairs, repaired the edges of doormats, or riveted broken china.

Seeing political performers on TV is tame compared with watching Parliamentary candidates beneath one's own window haranguing a crowd with local hecklers. I have three special memories of political activity, and the first was hearing my father say how Old So-and-so had gone to an election meeting and lost his head.

'Poor man,' I thought. 'He can't find it by himself because his eyes will have gone with it'. I was used to my dolls having similar misadventures, and to the nasty smell of Seccotine when the heads had been stuck on again, so after a few days I assumed that Old So-and-so's had been similarly restored as I heard no more about it. To me, heads were peculiar things. Watching Mother casually thrusting into the front of her hat pretty hatpins so long that their ends stuck out at the back, I used to wonder how old you had to be before a hole formed in your head to accommodate them. It was quite clear from her face that Mother felt no pain: I used to watch her carefully.

It must have been quite a few years later that I admired an election poster stuck on the wall by the blacksmith's behind the Other Chemist's shop, because I could read it and understand that it brought in the names of all three men who wanted to sit down in the Houses of Parliament. 'BEN NET the EARLY bird,' it said, 'and put in EDMONDSON with a big majority'. I thought that was very funny, and Major Edmondson did win the seat.

My third recollection belongs to the late 1930s, when Sir Oswald Mosley's Blackshirts put their case in the Square and called for supporters. With the speakers came three young men, very stiff and close-cropped in the Blackshirt uniform, who performed some brisk military movements and marched stiffly up and down. They looked quite sinister, but 'Not even enough of them to form fours,' scoffed a spectator who could remember the Kaiser's War.

When both the supermarket and its carpark had been rebuilt on the new road developed behind the Market Square, the gap which had held my old home became the entrance to nowhere. It is being filled in with new business premises, large enough to stretch right back down our yard as far as the pigsty where my sister and I declaimed *Julius Caesar* many summers ago, so a great many more people will be looking out of the windows to see what goes on in the Square. I shall still think of them as my windows.

Proclamation of His Majesty

KING GEORGE V.

At WITNEY, 10th MAY, 1910.

Order of Procession.

MOUNTED CONSTABLE.

WITNEY TOWN BAND.

MACE BEARER,
Attended by two Constables.

THE BAILIFF OF WITNEY,
(MR. C. STORY).

E CHAIRMAN OF THE URBAN DISTRICT COUNCIL (MR. E. TARRANT)
with the CLERK (MR R. F. CUTHBERT).

THE MEMBERS OF THE WITNEY URBAN DISTRICT COUNCIL.

THE CLERGY AND MINISTERS.

REPRESENTATIVES OF ADJOINING COUNCILS.

WITNEY FIRE BRIGADE.

RESIDENTS OF WITNEY.

THE FRIENDLY SOCIETIES.

Route of the Procession will be kept by The Boys' Brigade (Capt. J. H. Early), and
The Boy Scouts (Scout-Master Jones).

Proclamation of His Majesty King George V at Witney 10 May 1910. (WTR)

Procedure.

The Procession will be marshalled at Staple Hall at 12-15 p.m.

Fanfare sounded at 12-30, after which the Proclamation will be read by the Bailiff of Witney, concluding with the words " God save the King."   These words will be repeated by all present.   The National Anthem will then be sung, and the Bailiff will call for " Three Cheers for the King." Fanfare.

The Procession will then march to Parliament House, Corn Street, where the Proclamation will be read a second time with the same ceremony.

The Procession will then march to the Town Hall, where the Proclamation will be read a third time with the same ceremony.

The 'Procedure' for proclaiming George V as monarch in Witney on 10 May 1910. (PR)

24

ABOVE: The Proclamation by the Town Hall: a small bystander noticed that the man holding the horse's head did not take off his top hat when 'God Save the King' was played, but a timely toss of the horse's head neatly knocked it off for him. (WTR) BELOW: On Coronation Day, 22 June 1911, schoolchildren marched through the Square. (TW)

25

CORONATION DAY

THE 'F' COMPANY

4TH BATT. OXFORD & BUCKS. LIGHT INFANTRY

Will parade on Church Green at 11-45 a.m., when a

FEU-DE-JOIE

Will be fired

The following is published for the information of the Public :

A Feu-de-joie consists of the following movements :—Company drawn up in line; Firing commences from right hand man, running down the front and up the rear rank; Band plays portion of National Anthem; Two more rounds fired in similar manner; Band plays National Anthem; Following movements carried out :

FIX BAYONETS	ORDER ARMS
SLOPE ARMS	REMOVE HEAD-DRESSES
ROYAL SALUTE	THREE CHEERS
PRESENT ARMS	UNFIX BAYONETS
SLOPE ARMS	CLOSE RANK—MARCH

God save the King!

The military salute the new King. (PR)

WITNEY.

CELEBRATION

OF THE

Coronation

OF THEIR MAJESTIES

King George 5th & Queen Mary,

JUNE 22nd, 1911.

OLD PEOPLE'S DINNER

All Old People, being 60 years of age and upwards, and living in the rateable area of the Urban District of Witney, are requested to send in their names to the Committee, who will sit at the Corn Exchange for that purpose on Saturday, June 3rd, from 6-30 to 8 p.m.

SPORTS, Etc.

The Committee will sit in the Town Hall to receive entries for the following on Tuesday, June 13th, from 7 till 9 p.m ; or entries may be made to the gentlemen named before that date :

1.	BOWLS TOURNAMENT	*to*	MR. C. JACKSON.
2.	TENNIS TOURNAMENT	,,	MR. C. W. LIST.
3.	ADULT SPORTS	,,	MR. F. HAYTER.
4.	MARATHON RACE	,,	MR. F. HAYTER.
5.	DECORATED PREMISES	,,	MR. C. STORY.
6.	CROQUET TOURNAMENT	,,	MR. F. BROOKS.

Witney celebrates the 1911 Coronation. (PR)

LEFT: I am ready to join in the 1911 celebrations, and RIGHT: plod along with a flag. OPPOSITE: Father's shop in 1919. The lefthand side is let to Miss Parsons, who runs a needlework shop. Her sister, Mrs Cadel, has the toyshop on the other side of Mr Burton's. He was a hairdresser and tobacconist. For some years round about 1908, Mrs Burton was in charge of the Telephone Exchange — one small switchboard in a little room behind the shop. Few firms, and fewer households, had a phone: the number of Early's Blanket Mills was Witney 3. (All WTR)

OPPOSITE BELOW: The morning after the fire at the tailor's shop of Mr Fitz, 1911. Mr Walters sold jewellery on the right. To the left is one of several shops in the Market Square which used to belong to Messrs Valentine and Barrell. Later Mr Valentine ran a tailoring business on The Hill, where Mr Denis Green is to be found today, and in 1920 Mr Barrell built the premises for his mail order firm, The Witney Blanket Company, down The Leys. BELOW: Two years after the fire, Mr Huddleston built the cinema on the site. Mrs Huddleston, pianist of silent film days, is leaning against the central pillar. I used to watch long queues from my window but years later they dwindled and the Palace closed in 1985. (Both PB)

ABOVE: The Fire Brigade's Old Manual pump, put out Tarrant's shop fire on King George V's Coronation Day, stood in the Leys when his Silver Jubilee was celebrated there in 1935. (PR) BELOW: The two ends of the Square . . . High Street is at the bottom of The Hill. (PB)

ABOVE: Church Green is on the other side of the righthand buildings. The Cinema can be seen through the Town Hall pillars. BELOW: The turn into Corn Street shows through the pillars. (PB) Leigh's ironmongery is on the left of the corner and Tarrant's Wholesale Department on the right. (TW)

ABOVE: From a side window, I could see the edge of Church Green and, when the trees had shed their leaves, tell the time by the Church clock — in 1907. (PB) BELOW: Mrs Joan Ford (née Cadel, right) and her sister Mrs Mary Ford retired in 1971. Behind them is the shop which their parents took over from Mr Moore in 1913. The premises are now occupied by the Anglia Building Society. (MF)

Market Day

There was one day which announced itself to the Square by the sheer noise it made and that was Thursday, Market Day. From as far back as I can remember until after Hitler's War, my early morning was filled with the sound of wooden hurdles cascading to the ground from a handcart, one load after another. Then they were seized by the two Market Men, wearing sacking aprons with bunches of dirty cords thrust into the waist, who tied them together to form long rows of square pens, two deep. They left alleyways a hurdle's width between them, first for the animals when they were driven in, and then for the auctioneer and his crowd when the sale started.

I always admired the simplicity of these arrangements. When the sheep arrived, only one end of a hurdle had to be untied, so that it could be drawn aside into the alleyway like a door to the pen, while the cords at the other end obliged as hinges.

Then the animals began to appear, and pretty tired they looked. Sheep and cattle used to be driven in from the farms on foot. After a weary trudge along the roads they became confused in the streets and often brought confusion to both traffic and pedestrians. Cattle were taken to the yard behind the Post Office where I couldn't see them; sheep were herded into the alleyways and then divided among the pens, their bleating accompanied by barking and shouting, thwacks and thuds. Sometimes they were packed in so tightly that they could scarcely move. Steam rose from their bodies as did an unmistakable smell, and the smell increased as the day wore on.

This was not improved by the additional odour of pig. These animals arrived in carts and were hauled out indiscriminately by legs, tails, and ears, squealing vociferously until they were all enclosed in the rows over by the lamp-post in the middle, furthest from our window, for which we were thankful. They made more fuss than the sheep, for they had more reason to, and for some time after they'd been penned, stood shaking their heads sorrowfully until they'd forgotten the outrage done to their ears. The smell was quite appalling if you stopped to think about it, and was made far worse years later, about the time of Hitler's War, when it was joined by the smell of blood; on top of everything else, the wretched creatures' ears were punched with a metal clipper.

When animals were no longer driven along the road on foot but were all transported to market in vans, wheeled gangways with sides, and with ridges across them to prevent hooves from slipping, were used to bring sheep down to the ground, and I could never think why similar ones could not be used for pigs, to stop all the hauling about.

Often a pig escaped its tormentors and there was pandemonium until it was caught again. It would change direction more often than a hare, and there were as many ideas about catching it as there were people engaged on the job. Men scuffled this way and that, yelling 'Hu! Hu!', brandishing sticks or holding hurdles in attempts to stop the escape; small boys hurled themselves joyfully into the confusion, screaming as noisily as the pig. Everybody seemed to be enjoying it except the pig and me. We were always on the same side.

Sometimes a sheep showed some spirit by leaping unexpectedly over the hurdles and making a run for it. The Market Men always dealt with this, having first caught their sheep, by tying a couple of hurdles over the top of the pen, making a complete cage.

The market fascinated me so much that I had to watch it, but I never knew if I loved or hated it. Week after week, when I was not at school, I perched on the back of an old-fashioned sofa by the window and looked out, afraid of being horrified by what I saw and afraid of missing something interesting if I didn't look. You never knew what would happen next. Not only animals escaped.

Itinerant pedlars, cheapjacks, and entertainers in the truly medieval tradition would take advantage of the Market Day crowds. Some are only on the fringe of my memory and I recall most clearly the escapist who, swathed in padlocked chains and fiercely knotted ropes, would lie down on an old sack and writhe horribly on the ground until he had freed himself from their coils. However much enthusiasm had been put into his tying-up by the spectators who had accepted his challenge, he would free himself in the end, and an agonising process it looked. He seemed a very greasy person and at the time I thought he couldn't wash very often, but it has since occurred to me that the grease might have served a useful purpose. How much suffering was real and how much was part of the show is also open to question, but he groaned and wriggled and heaved, and pulled such dreadful faces that I felt sorry for him and almost put him in the same category as the pigs — almost, not quite. I felt sorrier for the pigs because I couldn't see anyone standing by to poke the man with a stick and force him to behave like that.

My sister was very much impressed by a travelling dentist, who set up his chair on a little platform and undertook to pull out teeth on the spot. There was no doubt about the suffering of his clients; she daren't look, but couldn't help hearing. The dentist called out to tell everybody how clever he was, and how highly qualified was the lady who helped him. She was dressed quite spectacularly as a nurse and her qualification, spoken of with great respect by the dentist, was that of being a doctor's daughter.

Other branches of medicine were not neglected as hawkers came along bringing cures for everything. Theirs was a wonderful patter, which soon drew a crowd to listen to the tale of dreadful diseases which could be cured by this one's pill or that one's potion. Doubters who challenged them would hear of the many testimonials written by grateful clients and, as soon as the first purchase had been sheepishly made, an increasing rush followed.

There was one such hawker whose patter had particularly entertained my father. This man sold pills which, according to him, cured almost every known ill and could be obtained from no one else. He must have done a good trade because later on he slipped into my father's shop to renew his stock, asking confidentially, 'Got any old pills you don't want, Mister? Don't matter what sort.'

My father sometimes spoke of another pill vendor who interested him, although this one had held forth in the Square in the 1840s, well before Father's time. He was a shepherd from nearby Curbridge, whose parents had taken him away from a Witney school at the age of eight, because the weekly wage the child could earn on a farm — one shilling and sixpence, or seven and a half new pence — was really needed by the family. He took an interest in herbs and, while still a young shepherd, became known locally as a chap able to treat all manner of ailments in sheep, other farm animals, and even human beings. This led to his making pills which he hawked around, visiting our Square on Market Days. Later he devoted himself to pill-making, left for Wigan and St Helens and made a fortune.

His name was Thomas Beecham, and his pills were sold in many parts of the world, advertised from the very beginning as 'worth a guinea a box'. These words caught people's fancy ten years ahead of the time when such slogans became popular. Guineas, each worth one pound and one shilling, sounded more elegant than pounds, and were in general use by professional men such as doctors and Harley Street specialists when they were stating their fees.

I find only the oldest of us recognise the slogan today, but if you ask for Beecham's Pills in a chemist's shop you will actually pay a guinea for them, though it is called one pound and five pence. Instead of a circular wooden box you will be handed a slender carton, and you will find that the pills have turned into tablets, each one in solitary confinement encased in a 'blister' or 'pop out pocket', but the packet is adorned with a coloured picture of the plant which produces aloes as this is still the main ingredient.

In the 1960s I found Thomas Beecham's great-grand-daughter, Anne Francis, on our doorstep and we enjoyed her purposeful visit.

She had come to Witney to find out anything she could relating to the pill-maker's early days, as she was writing his biography, later published under the title *A Guinea a Box*.

Market Day brought plenty of variety to the Square and I loved the general bustle, didn't pay much attention to the smell, but couldn't accept what was involved for the animals who had no choice like the tied-up man, and were more likely than not going to be killed afterwards. Driven in, penned, crushed together, they stood there for hours without food or water in sun, rain, or snow, prodded and poked by possible buyers while small boys wandered round haphazardly striking them with sticks. It was something to be worried over every week.

People were usually fun to watch, and on Thursdays there were plenty of all kinds. The Market Men linked all the patterns of the day together, from the setting up of the hurdles to the clearing up when they'd been taken down again. After the sheep had been penned, the drovers stood about with their dogs. My memory clothes most of them in drill coats and trousers which had once been white, and is certain of at least one smock. Their hats had lost most of their shape and all their colour, since they seemed to be soaked in grease, and their trousers were all tied beneath the knees with string. I was told this was to prevent rats running up their legs.

Ordinary people were there whether they had come to do business or not. Mothers brought small children who all wanted to pat the sheep, and then were afraid to do it after they'd been lifted up so that they could reach over the hurdles.

Farmers looked rather purposeful and frightening people to me in their breeches, gaiters and hard hats. I thought of them as having the power of life and death over animals, and so they were less dreadful than butchers, who had only the power of death. They prodded the sheep with sticks and plunged their hands into the fleece as they priced the animals, stood about talking and laughing in groups, went in and out of the Hotel and the Corn Exchange. Minute by minute the noise increased, and bleating and squealing, shouting and laughing built up to its crescendo in the market bell, announcing that the sale was about to begin. The bell was a big handbell, swung up and down like the one we were used to at school, but making far more noise.

Immediately the surging scene had a centre. The auctioneer had arrived. Farmers and butchers gathered round him, spectators followed them up and down the alleyways, a powerful new noise rose up and went on until the sale had finished. The auctioneer didn't waste a second. 'Twenty-two I'm bid, twenty-two I'm bid, twenty-three, twenty-four, twenty-five, twenty-six, twenty-seven, twenty-eight, any advance on twenty-eight, going, going, gone!' Bang came his fist down on his book, the sale was entered, then he and his entourage shuffled off along the alleyway to the next pen. 'Fifteen I'm bid, fifteen, sixteen, seventeen, any advance on seventeen . . .'

Often there were only pigs and sheep to be sold by auction in the Square, but now and then there were smaller creatures such as hens and rabbits, and these were enclosed in a stack of wire cages like miniature high-rise flats. Sometimes a horse or pony was walked up and down in the middle of a group of people before the bidding started, and this struck me as particularly sad, for it had probably been a friend of its owner in a way that pigs and sheep, even hens and rabbits, could never be. Sometimes there was a vehicle to be sold as well, such as a tub, a cart, or a trap. The collection of agricultural machinery set out on the high bank at the other side of the Square was never sold by auction; when the market was over, it was taken back to the shop of the ironmonger who had sent it there to be looked at. He was my grandfather, Alfred Leigh, and the shop is still there at the corner of Corn Street. Grandfather took it over from the uncle to whom he had been apprenticed — the quaintly-worded deed of apprenticeship hangs in the office to this day — and since Leigh & Sons is now run by his great-grandson, the shop has seen five generations of my mother's family.

On normal Market Days the whole Square in front of our home would be filled with pens, but twice a year the space along and behind the two blocks of buildings would be filled too. These occasions were the Christmas Fat Stock Market and Easter Lamb Market, when tiny bleats joined in the general hubbub. I tried not to think of these lambs at dinnertime on Easter Sunday, but in one sense the pretty little creatures had disappointed me; the first time I had been able to lean over the hurdles far enough to pat a lamb, I had expected its fleece to be soft — as soft as lambswool — and had been quite startled to find how harsh it was. I never wanted to fondle another, until I was invited to feed an orphan from a bottle on a farm. That was something quite different.

When the auction was over, drovers reappeared to take the animals away and often it was the dreaded butchers' men who came to drive them off. At least the pigs didn't have to go to their doom on foot for, with renewed squealing, they were hauled back into carts. Immediately there were empty pens, the Market Men started to untie the hurdles and stack them up on the handcart in toppling heaps which miraculously never fell right down.

As the Square emptied itself of animals and people, except for a remnant of small boys, the widespread filth could be seen and, as visible nastiness, appeared to release an even stronger smell. Week after week it looked as if the Square could never be clean again, but next came the liveliest part of the whole day, and the scene I enjoyed most. When those versatile performers, the Market Men, put on the last of their acts it was pure comedy.

37

They produced a large hose, connected it to a hydrant near our shop front and swilled the filth away. It rushed along the gutters to the iron gratings and gurgled down the drains.

This was what the small boys had been waiting for — I am not saying small persons, because I never saw a girl join in this fun. The hose was peppered with leaks from which quite tall and powerful jets of water soared in all directions. The boys ran through the jets with whoops of joy, tried to stop the leaks with their fingers or to re-direct the flow and squirt it on one another, and this usually ended in their getting wet themselves. The more daring would jump on the hose, trying to cut off the supply of water altogether. Their yells of delight were punctuated with the roars of the Market Men, who had put up with relays of troublesome small boys all day and had had enough. When really exasperated, the nozzle man would make threatening gestures with the nozzle itself but, though he directed the water near enough to the boys to splash them, he was careful not to let them feel its full force; this would probably have swept them off their feet and swirled them away too.

In spite of these young pests the Square would usually be clean and tidy again by teatime, when there was nothing to be seen but wetness, and the people who had to cross it picking their way carefully among the puddles.

Though I'd spent so much of the day being sorry for the living creatures sold out there, and never became reconciled to their plight, I was able to make some distinction between them and pet animals. For one thing, there were so many of them. Then the pigs smelt, the sheep did seem rather silly, and the cattle terrified me, not without cause.

After being driven in from the farms on foot they often became frantic as they were urged through the streets to the iron pens in the cattle yard. Goaded beyond endurance, they would make a bid for liberty, dash onto the pavement, find it more slippery than the road, and discover the world was full of two kinds of people; there were those who ran away and those who stood their ground, flapping their arms and urging the animal to go in any other direction than the one it wanted to. The sight of a bullock apparently wanting to toss you is alarming, and it is no less so when the creature suddenly skids round on a narrow pavement to face the opposite direction, snorting in terror itself.

I must have been under five years old when Mother and I were chased along the pavement in the High Street by a bullock being driven to market. Whenever I think of it now, I see it from the outside, and picture something like the Tenniel drawing of Alice in Wonderland running hand in hand with the Red Queen, being urged to go 'Faster! Faster!' and having no feet on the ground at all. That was how I felt when we raced along a few yards of pavement, which seemed to go for miles, before we could run through a doorway festooned with scrubbing brushes to take refuge in the Penny Bazaar. Now, it didn't need an animal to chase me in there on ordinary days, for it was an Aladdin's Cave of golden pennyworths. My choice always fell on one of the gilt filigree prams, mangles, pushchairs, motor cars, motor bikes and other delights, small enough to be cradled lovingly in the palm of the hand yet having wheels which really turned. Even one of these treasures didn't make me forget we had been chased; for years afterwards I was frightened of the most peaceful cow, and not until I had grown up did the fear suddenly leave me, early one morning in camp.

No Guide myself, in spite of my Girl Guide games in the garden, I had been asked to join a camp to look after the swimming. I didn't take a pop-gun or any bows and arrows, but I did take an umbrella, and gathered from the giggles which greeted me that a strange female turning up so equipped was one of the funniest sights the Company had yet seen. They were to see an even stranger one.

I woke up in a bell tent early the next morning to hear a fumbling, chewing and snorting nearby, and peeped underneath the canvas flap to find the camp was being invaded by cows. Into my mind leapt an horrific picture of pandemonium as guy ropes snapped and children were trampled into a tangle under the canvas before they were properly awake.

Family lore held a story of how Mother had once protected my sister and herself from a runaway bullock by opening an umbrella in its face; this had brought it slithering to a standstill while they, too, took refuge in a shop. I slid out of my sleeping-bag, put on my wellingtons, seized my only weapon, crept out of the tent, and opened my umbrella in the face of the nearest cow, very gently, as I didn't want a stampede.

I didn't know what to expect, but it worked. Instantly the whole herd stopped munching and looked up, backed away, turned, and trotted peacefully to the top of the field and through a gate which had been left open. I closed it, rejoicing. Those girls who had also been roused by the quiet movements of the cows, and had peeped out of their tents, were rewarded by the sight of the stranger in their midst, wearing wellingtons and pyjamas and armed with the umbrella, wandering over the landscape in the wake of those very placid cows.

It made a good story at breakfast, the umbrella was adopted as mascot and took part in various Camp Fire entertainments, while I wondered why I had been so frightened of cattle.

Shopkeepers in the town were used to their premises being used as bolt holes, and it was not only human beings who burst into their shops. A sheep once bolted into ours and was not very happy about it. Nor were we. It is not easy to persuade a sheep to turn round when it has wedged itself between the end of a counter and a cupboard, is contemplating itself in a mirror, and not liking what it sees. Nor is it easy to show it the door when the doorway is completely blocked by people from outside crowding in to take a look. We were glad to bid it goodbye.

I should like to have been in Cook and Boggis's, the drapers' shop at the far end of the Square, when an assistant who happened to be perched up a ladder with her back to the door gave her usual greeting to customers approaching her counter, and then turned round to find she had said, 'May I help you, Madam?' to a cow.

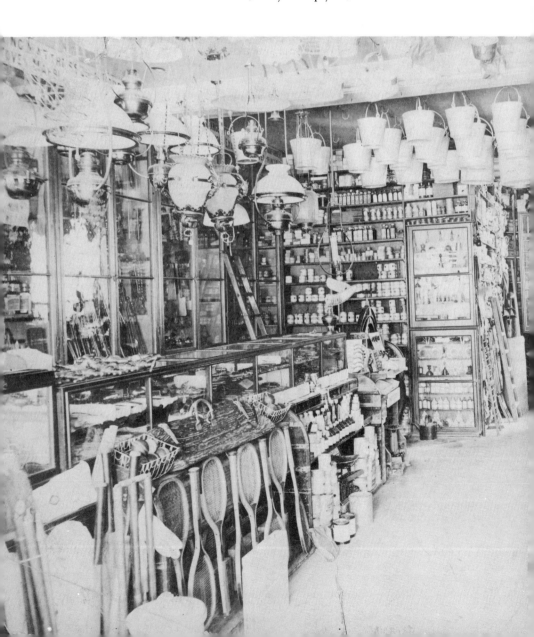

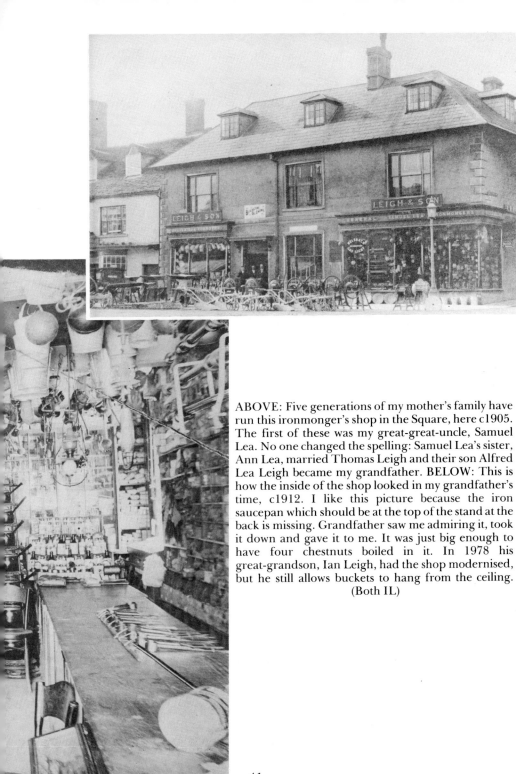

ABOVE: Five generations of my mother's family have run this ironmonger's shop in the Square, here c1905. The first of these was my great-great-uncle, Samuel Lea. No one changed the spelling: Samuel Lea's sister, Ann Lea, married Thomas Leigh and their son Alfred Lea Leigh became my grandfather. BELOW: This is how the inside of the shop looked in my grandfather's time, c1912. I like this picture because the iron saucepan which should be at the top of the stand at the back is missing. Grandfather saw me admiring it, took it down and gave it to me. It was just big enough to have four chestnuts boiled in it. In 1978 his great-grandson, Ian Leigh, had the shop modernised, but he still allows buckets to hang from the ceiling.

(Both IL)

41

Around 1906, Thursdays were busy days. These two
pictures show the four sides of the Square's middle
part. Our shop (top, right) was opposite the
Marlborough Hotel (below) and Mr Neave's faced the
draper's shop of Messrs Cole and Crawley (below, left)
part of the other detached block of buildings in the
Square, in 1914. (Both TW)

The Corn Exchange

Our neighbour, the Corn Exchange, was a two-storeyed Victorian building showing a brave face to the Square. Its railings came down during Hitler's War and were contributed to something vague called the War Effort, and its balcony, which I had never seen supporting anything heavier than draped bunting, came down in the interests of safety, making it look a little more bald than before. Moreover, it was doomed to stand empty for a number of years, waiting for its fate to be decided. Happily it has now been restored and is in use as a public hall again.

It seemed to me as a child that all events took place either outside in the Square or inside in the Corn Exchange, so I was doubly lucky. From a side window upstairs I could watch people going in and out and, if there were something grnad like a dance, the ladies would have ribbons or feathers in their hair, and sometimes the ribbons glittered with diamonds, which I knew could be bought by the yard. I should have liked some, even though they weren't as splendid as Queen Mary's. The building bounded the yard which led to our garden, so I could put my ear to the ventilation grids and try to make out what was happening, and from the garden itself could sometimes see people at the dressing-room windows behind the stage. With any luck they would be in fancy dress and have paint on their faces.

Every Market Day farmers went into the main hall, and what could they be doing there but exchanging corn? I thought the process must be rather like ours when we swopped pencils, pen-holders and rubbers at school. They had desks, too, which were stacked up against the walls for the rest of the week.

Over the years the hall was used for concerts and auctions, plays and dances, distribution of bread and beef under the terms of an old charity, Twelfth Night children's parties, British Legion dinners, political meetings and voting, trade fairs and exhibitions, Speech Days, dog and bird shows, the League of Health and Beauty, Musical Festivals, military billets and much besides. There was a room used for wedding receptions, where meetings of the Board of Guardians and Town Council had formerly taken place. How I had loved the stately arrival of a Lady Guardian who was driven up in her own carriage! Her coachman had a cockade in his hat and always walked the horse round and round the Square and up and down the Green, until it was time for her stately departure.

I think I first became aware of the building as a place of entertainment and not simply as a boundary to my territory when a Musical Society performed *Elijah* there one afternoon. I couldn't imagine what it looked like inside, but there were a lot of people singing together, then a lady or gentleman singing alone, and it all made a pleasant background to my game with a heap of gravel which had just arrived. Then certain passages entranced me and I put my ear to a ventilation grid. Never had I dreamed a lady's voice could soar so high, and I startled Mother by rushing into the kitchen to tell her so.

Years later, when I was standing on Mount Carmel rejoicing in the view of the Holy Land spread around and below me, Mendelssohn's music mixed with memories of the gravel heap flooded my mind. 'Oh Baal, hear us . . .'

It was suitable that I should have been captivated by music coming from the Corn Exchange. My mother and father had been violinists in an amateur orchestra and, when they were at a practice there, a string snapped on Mother's violin so Father fixed it for her. That was how they met. It is a sobering thought that one can owe one's very existence to so slight a circumstance as a broken violin string.

Mother was married from her home over the ironmonger's shop in the Square in 1901, a week after Queen Victoria died. It would have been thought more becoming to postpone the wedding but, as it had been twice postponed because of illness, no one was in a mind to put it off again. When Mother described the ceremony years later, it always sounded as if, at the first sight of the bride's carriage, mourning had been whipped down from the Methodist Chapel and replaced almost before she had reached the pavement on the way out.

Her going-away costume sadly acknowledged that the whole country was in mourning, and I think she would be greatly surprised to know that the little dove-grey jacket, which she never really liked, is now in the Museum of Costume at Bath.

When Mother was 88 and we were looking at some old family wedding groups, I asked her: 'Why haven't I seen any of your wedding photographs? Whatever happened to them?'

'Oh, my dear,' she said, 'Of course we didn't have any taken. Why, the Queen had only just died!'

I stared at her in amazement. She was laughing, but it was clear that not only as a young Victorian woman had she accepted that photography was too frivolous to be indulged in after the death of the Queen. She was not quarrelling with that view over sixty years later.

44

For years I believed that the most outstanding entertainment ever given in the Corn Exchange was a local production called *Britannia's Revue*. It raised money for the Red Cross during the Kaiser's War and was particularly enthralling to me because my own sister was in it, as well as a lot of other people I knew. So was my uncle's brass fire helmet. Britannia wore it.

A very beautiful and dignified young woman sat on the stage all the time the curtain was up, and she looked just like the Britannia on the back of a penny, only better, because of the colour. She held a shield and trident, wore white draperies with a Union Jack cloak, and my uncle's brightly polished helmet which had a red frill along the top for the occasion.

People came to visit her throughout the evening, all to pay homage and most of them to dance or sing, or both. First of all came the British Isles. A young aunt of mine danced the Highland Fling in a proper kilt and two other performers danced the Welsh and Irish jigs. The colonies were there and I specially remember a lady who wore a splendid purple sari and sang one of the Indian Love Lyrics — *Pale hands I loved* . . . Then there were people who weren't quite real, like John Bull and History and Father Time. Hope was a big girl from my school who was also draped in white, and had a gold anchor. She had a little bit to say, then nothing more to do but stand there looking pretty.

Then there was the English Rose who danced accompanied by four Rosebuds, each holding half a wooden hoop entwined with paper roses. This was really thrilling for I had seen one of the arches being made, I knew all the Rosebuds, and one of them was my sister. The local paper must have liked it too because it said, in print, that this was one of the best items of the evening and 'it fairly took the audience by storm and again and again an encore was demanded'.

There were the Allies — France, Russia, Belgium, Serbia, Japan, Italy and Roumania. Notable among them were two ladies in red, yellow and black dresses almost ripped to pieces to show what a bad time Gallant Little Belgium had had. One of the two was my aunt, playing her second part, and she hadn't liked being obliged to tear the dress all over so badly after carefully making it. Italy had a tambourine which I should have liked. The Armed Forces were represented by Tommy Atkins, who sang, I think, and Jack Tar, who danced a few steps of the Hornpipe. His sister, the English Rose, told me recently that he had refused to 'make a fool of himself' by dancing it all the way through. There wasn't a Royal Air Force then, just a Royal Flying Corps; aviators belonged either to the Army or the Navy, so a lady danced as an Aeroplane and the paper said this was done 'in a particularly skilful manner, which met with due recognition'.

There were other kinds of people helping with the war — familiar ones such as the Red Cross Nurse, as well as those exciting

45

newcomers, the Munition Girl and the Farm Girl. At the end there was a big group on the stage and it would have been bigger if some performers hadn't played two, or even three, parts. Britannia and the audience had seen a gathering almost as comprehensive in its way as that in the Scottish War memorial of the future, in Edinburgh Castle, but it was not quite so all-embracing, because Britannia received no homage from horses, dogs or pigeons. Right at the end Peace came on, wearing a beautiful pair of big white wings, and afterwards the paper said all the 'numerous artistes sustained their parts in an exceptionally capable manner'.

Probably this performance accounts for my always having regretted that there is no real national costume for those who, like the first Elizabeth, proudly proclaim themselves to be 'mere English'. The Scot has his kilt, the Welshwoman her tall hat, the Japanese the kimono and the Indian his feathers, but the best the English can do in a national pageant is to appear either as Britannia or John Bull, and both these symbols are rather out of date.

The next year I was thought old enough to take part in a Red Cross Concert myself, so I became a dancer overnight. Eight children danced together and I was among the smallest four, dressed as Pierrettes in white with black bobbles. My sister was among the tallest four and they had a rather pyjama-like garment. With royal blue trousers and tunics they had floppy blue berets and floppy black ties, and were unaccountably called French Artists.

We pranced about to a tune called *In the Shadows*, sometimes playing a kind of Follow my Leader, and sometimes standing in a more or less straight line kicking our legs this way and that. At the end the Artists sank down on one knee so that the Pierrettes could sit on the other one. At least, that's what had happened at rehearsals, but on the night my Artist sank onto the wrong knee so that I had to squat on the air. No one seemed to mind, because we weren't left out when eight pottery money-box pigs were handed up after the final curtain. The grown-up ladies had boxes of chocolates or bouquets of flowers, which I thought very grand, but I still have my piggy bank intact.

There wasn't a Red Cross Concert the next year. The war was over and everybody knew there was never, never, going to be another one. The Corn Exchange was still used for all kinds of entertainment, only now it was real actors who came, not pretend ones like the people I knew. The 'Roosters' appeared — they had been a famous wartime Concert Party and were heard in the early days of radio. Every now and then a touring party presented such time-honoured dramas as *Maria Marten, or the Murder in the Red Barn* and *East Lynne*. I wasn't taken to these, so could only enjoy watching the people who did go, and listening to the actor who stood on the pavement calling loudly in a refined voice, 'Early doors! Early doors now open!' for about an hour before the curtain went up. When I was old enough to take myself I enjoyed *The Ghost Train,* the evergreen comedy-thriller written by the grand old warrior Private Godfrey of *Dad's Army,* alias Arnold Ridley, but I do wish I'd seen those old melodramas played for all they were worth in the days before people decided they were funny.

Father took us to see a conjuror because, in a sense, our shop was his partner. This magician put some water into a clear glass decanter, then offered to pour from it into clear glass tumblers any beverage the audience liked to name. Perhaps he couldn't hear very well, because he didn't always agree with me about which drink was being called for, but he poured out a rich red wine, tea, a foaming beer, and milk. My sister and I hugged ourselves with joy as we watched the little flick of the wrist with which he turned round the flask so that the water could run over the different chemicals smeared on its lip. Where had those chemicals come from but our shop? He had a lot of other tricks besides, like smashing watches borrowed from the audience and then returning them whole, or putting swords through a lady in a box without hurting her, but nothing held our attention like the pouring of those beverages. Father would never tell us what the chemicals were. 'Not my secret,' he'd say.

Why do we not have an Arts League of Service now? In the twenties this enterprising company visited towns like ours, bringing good entertainment where there was no theatre. I used to watch their huge van draw up just outside the Corn Exchange and the scenery, properties and dress baskets being carried in. As I looked forward so eagerly from one visit to the next I'm surprised I can recall only one item, the presentation of a song.

> 'Jackie boy!
> Master?
> Sing you well?
> Very well.
> Hey down, ho down,
> Derry derry down,
> Among the leaves so green-o.'

A teenage Hermione Baddeley, dressed in green as a page, sat cross-legged responding in mime to the words, and I can still see her flinging her head back in mischievous silent laughter at:

'The first one he shot at he missed,'. After all her triumphs, is that a gesture Miss Baddeley would have wished to be remembered by?

When any of us were watching an audience going into the Corn Exchange there was nearly always a moment at which the cry came, 'Everything will be all right now! She's here!' This meant that Old Sue had arrived, whom we had grown to think of as a kind of mascot. She turned up at almost every public hall in the town when she knew something was afoot, and I don't think she was ever

47

turned away, but given a seat and a share in the refreshments if there were any. Everybody knew her and no one minded if, after she had eaten her fill, she took a bite out of yet another cake or sandwich and said, 'Ah, pity to waste it,' as she stowed it away in the folds of her garments.

For all the many years I knew her, Old Sue seemed truly old. A little bent old bundle of black clothes which looked as if they never came off, she would have been taken for a witch at once by anyone meeting her in a fairy tale, but in real life she was usually to be seen harmlessly sitting about in odd corners, or looking through dustbins. You might meet her anywhere, and in the Square her usual perches were on the bank opposite our shop or on the steps underneath the roof of the Buttercross. People used to put things in the dustbins for her to find, well wrapped up, but if Sue found anything which in her judgement was too good to be thrown away, she would go to the house or shop and ask if she might take it.

Old Sue had her regular places of call. Health problems she brought to Father, who provided what he hoped would help her, and he was once gratified to hear her say to a passerby as she left our shop, 'Gen'rous bloke in thur. I arsked un for a lolly for me cough and 'e gin I a 'ole 'andful. Black uns!' she ended triumphantly, waving the packet.

Whenever she had trouble with her shoes she came to Mother because 'I reckons me fet be the same size as yourn,' but she could never be persuaded to take more than one shoe at a time. 'T'other un be good yet,' she would insist, handing the unwanted one back, so Mother would store it away ready for the next visit. Sue had strong opinions about accepting help. She told Mother that a certain lady had offered to give her a meal whenever she liked to ask for it but, said Sue, 'I never goes where they makes coffins.'

At one time the Marlborough Hotel in the Square gave her some dinner every day, asking her to take her own plate, and this led to her coming to Father in some distress with a difficult problem. 'Can you give I summut to stop I falling down?' she asked. 'I be allus falling and now I've broke me plate.' Father gave this some thought. He had to say he didn't think anyone could prevent her falling, but 'I tell you what, Miss Collier,' he said, 'I'll give you something which will make it less serious for you when you do fall,' and he fetched her a large enamel plate from our picnic set.

Poor old Sue. At least, living the life she did, she kept her independence; she was not homeless, and it may have been a much better life that she was leading inside her own head. As she went about muttering to herself I once distinguished the words 'S'pose I'd better put on me best black silk dress tonight.'

Between the wars there were regular Saturday night dances in the Corn Exchange which I have good reason to remember. Through some freak of acoustics it always sounded as if the Jazz Band were up my bedroom chimney, so I was glad that the Saturday night hops stopped on the stroke of midnight, like Cinderella.

Towards dusk one evening, when Mother was thinking it was time to stop weeding, a hoarse voice came from behind the gooseberry bushes. 'Can you hide me?' it said.

Mother was startled but kept her wits about her and replied, 'That all depends on what you've done.'

A shamefaced young man popped up and explained that he'd slipped out of the dance and climbed over our wall because the dances were out of bounds to undergraduates, and the hall was being raided by the Proctor and his Bulldogs.

Mother took him up the yard and into our sitting-room, where he was able to peep out between the curtains and watch his companions down in the Square either being questioned or slipping away, but he was uneasy and slipped away himself as soon as he thought the coast was clear. We should have liked to know what happened to him. Father thought he had little chance of escape because, at that time, the few cars belonging to Oxford undergraduates carried a special green light to distinguish them from other people's, but I don't suppose it was impossible to disconnect those lights.

Soon after Hitler's War started, soldiers were billeted in the Corn Exchange, and our house and shop became a kind of annexe. We never knew what we should be asked to do next. One soldier had his letters addressed to us as he didn't expect to receive his mother's postal orders if they went to the Army Office. Another asked us to look after his pocket money and allow him to spend only so much a week, so we kept it in a tobacco tin in our safe with a balance sheet. On the day they were all innoculated, so many soldiers wandered into the shop looking sorry for themselves and vaguely in want of comfort that we ended with our large sitting-room full of them, mostly lying on the floor surrounding my father, who sat in the middle convalescing from a heart attack.

A sentry stamped up and down all night on our pavement, which was somehow reassuring, but when Father was very ill I ventured to ask him if stamping could be done quietly, and he found that it could.

Our relations with their commanding officer were less harmonious. He told us that the room on the second floor was to be turned into a canteen and asked politely if the wastepipe from the sink could discharge into the drain in our yard. When we hesitated, foreseeing trouble with what was evidently going to be a Heath Robinson contrivance, he became less agreeable and asked if we should prefer to have the whole premises commandeered so that he could do what he liked with them. We gave in, but the frequent blocking of the drain became such a nuisance that we appealed to the Town Surveyor, who promptly gave us a piece of his mind for letting the Army get anywhere near his sewage system. According to him, that was the one thing the military could not touch. We had no idea of the sacrosanct nature of drains and told him of the officer's veiled threat. The Surveyor uttered words which could best be summarised as 'Stuff and nonsense' and in no time had the trespassing piece of pipe hoisted out of our drain.

Another side product of the canteen must have been the mouse which came through into my bedroom. Accustomed as I had been to the many antics into which the enquiring minds of my pet mice, Jehu, Jericho and Jehosaphat led them, I was still astonished at this one's activity. I sat up in bed and watched fascinated as he noisily explored the fireplace, walked the plank along the fire-irons in the fender, examined the trinkets on the dressing-table, and the oddments on top of the bookcase. For a time he sat washing his whiskers on the top of a sloping photograph up there, then put a tentative foot on the glass and slid down like a child in a playground. I suppose it gave him pleasure, for he climbed up and slid down the slope again and again. He had gone when I woke up next morning and that was the last I saw of him; I do hope he didn't have too disagreeable an end.

Eventually other billets were found for the soldiers and, when the Corn Exchange became our public hall once more, they were glad to join in the dances. If they had looked in at a pub or two on their way, who could be surprised? Some of those who were turned out for being a nuisance naturally tried to force their way in again. They had only to go down the Corn Exchange Yard, cross a cottage garden behind it, climb our high wall and walk up our yard. If by this time they had lost all sense of direction they would try to break into our kitchen; if not, they would try to climb through the window of the cloakroom which was exactly opposite, above our large rainwater butt.

One night when I was locking up I found a pair of paratroopers out there. One was very drunk, but the other one had fallen into the rainwater butt and was the better for it. I was quite frightened, but they meekly allowed me to show them out into the Square.

Then a thought struck me, and I called at a venture into the utter blackness of wartime, 'Come on out, the rest of you.' I was startled when three Red Devils popped up from behind some shrubs, and amazed to find them quite scared of me and glad to creep back to the reassuring company of their mates. By this time my knees felt like cotton wool, but I soon became used to these visitations. Sometimes the soldiers took me for the dance hall caretaker and tried to browbeat me into letting them back. It was no use trying to explain anything, but fairly simple to lead them to our heavy wooden doors and shut them out in the Square.

One morning, instead of getting the breakfast, and feeling remarkably foolish, I went out to look for a policeman and was lucky enough to find a well-known special constable on duty by the Buttercross. 'What would you do,' I asked him, 'if you found your kitchen window, back door and doorstep, smothered with blood? Wipe it up or tell the police?'

'Don't touch it, don't touch it,' he said urgently, and together we examined the stains, then went through the yard, garden, and all the outhouses, especially the woodshed, looking for something nasty. Nothing was to be found, so Mr Buckle went off to pursue his enquiries and I returned to the kitchen to get the breakfast. He came back later with the solution to the mystery, once again the story of a drunken soldier trying to find his way back into the dance hall. This one had given up and gone instead to a late night cafe where they dressed the hand he'd badly gashed when climbing our high wall. No wonder, as by this time the Army had topped it with a coil of barbed wire.

'Everything's all right now, so you can clean up,' said the policeman, and a thoroughly disagreeable job it was, taking far longer than it ever does in the whodunits. There and then I resolved never to commit murder by any means which produces blood.

Eventually the wholesale shedding of blood came to an end, on first the European, and then the Far Eastern Front; the Corn Exchange flew a flag from its balcony again and went back to peacetime pursuits.

An Old Time Dancing Class flourished there, and so did plays and pantomimes by an Amateur Dramatic Society still very much alive today. Bob Arnold sang with his own Concert Party. That was before the veil was lifted on the goings-on of the Archers at Ambridge, where he has not stopped singing. There can be very few Squares able to boast of having had white lines painted in them by so well-known a game-keeper, and it is said that he painted a white line all along the road to Burford, a distance of seven miles, which was joyfully described by his mates as being crooked all the way.

Sadly the Corn Exchange fell foul of the authorities for a series of misdemeanours, such as blowing a gasket in its boiler, possessing a floor which was breaking up, being in need of re-wiring, and not conforming to fire regulations, so the key was turned on it and there it stood, quiet and miserable.

When the Government decided that the country no longer needed Territorials under any name to defend it, the Drill Hall down the Corn Exchange Yard became redundant, was re-trained and found new employment as successor to the Corn Exchange itself. It has a most unglamorous approach but the Yard is not ashamed of this as it has always been busy. Among many other activities it gave a home to the Fire Station for as long as this was needed.

In readiness for its first motor engine, the Fire Brigade took over the Old Malt House down there, which had provided our garden with some rich smells and probably a few of those legendary rats. It was a fine addition to the excitement under my window when the fire engine dashed out into the Square, on its way to fight those fires which the local paper was wont to call 'calamitous conflagrations'. Room was also found for the Old Manual pumping engine, semi-retired since it was still used in the training course.

This old favourite had lived in High Street. It was drawn by two horses, was lit by candles in brass lanterns, announced its coming by the jingling of brass bells on the horses' harness as well as by the galloping of their hooves, and had water pumped from it by a team of eight men, four a side, through a leather hose with copper rivets. For a number of years the two horses were owned by Mr Payne, the local carrier, who drove them himself, and this was great good fortune because it is on record that in 1879 a mop factory was destroyed by fire because 'two engines arrived too late, one having been delayed by the refusal of two individuals to lend horses to draw it'.

The Old Manual, which I had first seen giving a good account of itself on George V's Coronation Night, made what was probably its last public appearance on a lovely day in May 1935, when the country celebrated his Silver Jubilee. Standing quietly by the churchyard wall bordering the Leys where Witney was rejoicing, the veteran received the respectful homage of every passerby who knew what it was.

On this occasion a successor had been called upon to play a more lively rôle. The mock house built of canvas over a wooden frame was quite impressive. It was planned that a fire should start in the chimney and, after a suitable pause, the Brigade go into action by rescuing an old lady and putting out the flames, which should entertain the crowd for about twenty minutes. Everything went wrong. The 'old lady' lit a smoke canister under the chimney, put a match to some straw and then had to run for her life as the whole thing blazed up, cackling with laughter. It was all over in about twenty seconds and the 'old lady' nearly had her pinny scorched.

Poor Old Manual. Instead of going out in a blaze of glory it was lost sight of and forgotten, pushed behind the buildings in the Corn Exchange Yard, while a younger engine was covering itself with glory helping to fight the fires of Hitler's blitz in Coventry, Birmingham and Bristol, London, Exeter and Portsmouth, and anywhere else where it was needed. When the war had been fought and won, and people had time to take an interest in the small things belonging to our past, someone went to search for the Old Manual and found a heap of rotten wood. Every scrap of metal had vanished. It was believed that some enterprising person, to whom everyone could give the same whispered name, had sold it all for scrap, in which case the venerable pump had probably played a part in winning the war when scrap metal was needed for arms.

It now seems extraordinary that the town depended on the Old Manual until 1928, when it was found unable to deal with a fire in the glove factory just outside the boundary. In that year our first motor fire brigade engine was bought and we were proud of it. Admittedly it was secondhand, a 1911 model whose newness had had time to wear off but, for many whom I heard speaking of it, that only added to its value and its glamour. Just think where its ripe experience had been gained! Where but in London? In 1928 London was still a magic word and a mysterious place, a long sixty miles away, and what was good enough for London yesterday was good enough for many of our tomorrows. We saw for another nine years its bright dash out into the Square and its more slow and soiled return.

The Manual had looked fine behind the two horses, but here was a Leyland engine with the power of 85 galloping steeds. Some of the Brigade admitted that it was awkward to handle, but those solid tyres were accustomed to hard city streets, not to the muddy roads and soft fields leading to the ricks and barns and old country cottages which were what the firemen expected to find ablaze. So many rick fires were attended that the secretary of our Brigade was content to describe one in the Log Book with the laconic words: 'One boy, one firework, one rick, one fire'. This was a change from the style indulged in by the local paper in earlier times when it described 'one of the most calamitous conflagrations that has ever taken place in this district. On Friday night last, as the good people of this quiet town were about to retire to bed, suddenly there burst upon the stillness of the night the most alarming cry of "Fire!" . . . Fireman Payne put his horses along in such fine style that in six minutes the Brigade was at work . . . Our Fire Brigade were perfectly calm in the most exciting circumstances . . . Fireman Tarrant narrowly escaped serious injury by the falling of a wall but fortunately only sustained a battered helmet'.

By then a veteran, our first motor engine was last seen at the beginning of the Second World War down by the Oxford Canal, ready to be used as an emergency pump, and it was our second motor, no more than two years old, which went to work in the blitzed cities, has since been carefully and lovingly restored by the firemen, lives proudly in the new Fire Station in a new road, and can always be relied upon to raise money for good causes.

The Corn Exchange Yard misses the bustle the Fire Brigade used to bring there and its leap out into the Square through a group of magnetised bystanders, but one way and another was kept busy even when its discarded and moribund neighbour, the Corn Exchange, was waiting for the scaffolding which came after many years to embrace her and bring the kiss of life.

PIGS PAY YOUR RENT!!!
By Using

RANSOM'S

ALTERATIVE
PIG POWDERS

These Powders are strongly recommended by many influential Breeders as being the best remedy that can be given for bringing them into good condition; they give tone to the stomach, increase the appetite and purify the blood from all gross and impure humours, producing a clear skin, thereby removing all that scurvy or scaly-like appearance which is so disagreeable to the eye and injurious to the animal.

The occasional use of these Powders is a preventive to any of the following diseases:—INFLAMMATION OF THE LUNGS, APOPLEXY AND INFLAMMATION OF THE BRAIN, MEASLES, MANGE, QUINSY, SWINE FEVER, &c.

DIRECTIONS.

A tea-spoonful to a table-spoonful may be given, according to the age of the animal, two or three times a week, in their usual food.

Tins, 1/- each; Three for 2/6.

Ransom's POULTRY SPICE

A Tonic Powder for use as a general stimulant, and a special excitant of the egg-producing organs. It produces a high condition of health and early maturity. For rearing Chickens and young birds it is without an equal.

DIRECTIONS.—To each 15 or 20 birds mix one table-spoonful in their soft warm food. To be given three or four times each week.   **1/- Tins; Three for 2/6.**

Ransom's TONIC CONDITION POWDER, for Horses.

Prepared only by
W. T. RANSOM, M.P.S., Agricultural Chemist, WITNEY.

This leaflet was probably used to wrap up small purchases. I used to think it an insult to pigs. Can you spot the spelling mistake? (PR)

Behind The Big Bottles

Anyone who speaks to me about my old home in the Square never fails to mention 'those lovely big bottles' — the three great carboys which stood on a high shelf in the shop window, above the goods on display. I wonder how much longer these symbols of the chemist's trade will last. With the barber's striped pole, disappearing, and the pawnbroker's three golden balls, which hard times are said to be bringing back again, they are the last survivors of the ancient signs which proclaimed a man's occupation to the world in the days when few people could read or write.

Perhaps some will return, now we rely so much on television and on picture strips to tell a story instead of on the printed word, especially as it has so recently been realised that a frightening number of people can neither read nor write today.

Our three carboys were filled with distilled water to which colouring had been added. Usually one was green, one red and one yellow, but they changed since Father loved experimenting with chemicals to produce different shades. Distilled water had to be used; with tap water the contents would soon have become cloudy, and the beauty of the colours lost.

Customers constantly asked questions about the carboys and were surprised to hear that they had once served the useful purpose of advertising the apothecary's trade, that we treasured them because we loved their beauty and liked to keep up a tradition. There was a widespread notion that we kept medicine in them, though I can't think why it should have been imagined that we put it in such an unsuitable and inconvenient place. How did people suppose we poured it out? One short-sighted customer, rightly believing he saw movement in the jars, asked, 'Have you got goldfish in there?' but children used to stand and gaze with rapt attention, for they knew what the movement was.

In the lovely curves of each jar was reflected the colourful life of the Square. Tiny people walked by, minute cyclists whizzed past, little red country 'buses drew away in a lordly manner, cars which crossed the Square to turn swelled and shrank grotesquely as they approached the jars and turned away, and the glory of it was that everything was upside-down.

It was useful to have children's attention held in a shop full of breakable bottles within reach, and as long ago as 1801 Maria Edgeworth told in *The Purple Jar* the story of a little girl who was fascinated by a jar in a chemist's window. As part of her education, Rosamund was allowed to buy it instead of spending the money on having her uncomfortable shoe mended by Mr Sole, the shoemaker, and made to keep to her bargain until the end of the month. By that time the child had become disillusioned with her purchase; when she had poured the purple liquid away because of its disagreeable smell, the 'vase' was seen to be a plain glass jar.

By the end of the month, little Rosamund wore shoes in which she could neither run, jump, dance, nor finally, walk; she was always too late to see anything she was called to look at, and on the very last day of the month her father refused to take her out with her brother because she was not neat.

My surprise at so harsh a punishment for preferring beauty to comfort is matched by my surprise at the chemist's readiness to part with his bottle, and at the servant's being able to carry it home so casually with the rest of the shopping without having a purple shower bath and an armful of shattered glass.

Our carboys, of blown glass, thick at the neck and almost paper thin at the curves, were so fragile that, for over thirty years, my father had allowed no one to dust them but himself. For the next twenty years it was I who held my breath as I dusted them. Father knew a chemist who had smashed such a carboy by inadvertently touching it, quite lightly, with the corner of a cardboard showcard.

Now and then I gingerly lifted out the great glass stoppers and washed them one by one. Came the day when the middle jar had been left unstoppered for a few minutes and a fly committed suicide in the coloured water. It was some time before we discovered the corpse, when our attention had been attracted by the cloudiness of the water and by a fungoid growth stretching down like an inverted mushroom. It took my sister and me an entire evening to clean it up.

First we had to syphon out the water through a rubber tube and carry it away in bucketsful. Next, with one of us perched on a ladder, we contrived to lift down the great jar so that we could clean it. Neither of us breathed freely until we had set it safely back on its strong stand. Then it was a simple matter of running up the ladder with about five gallons of distilled water, a jugful at a time, and restoring the tawny colour we favoured.

Fragile as they were, they survived two World Wars, though the plate glass window was broken twice. One night during the Kaiser's conflict, a young officer, merry with drink, found a satisfying use for his swagger cane. After leaving one of the dances in the Corn Exchange, he struck our window, and was so delighted with the resulting crash that he continued to aim at windows along the Square and out into High Street, until somebody managed to stop him.

The next morning he came in, very contrite, with a policeman and his cheque book. I don't know how many windows he had left cracked or broken, but it must have been a costly night's entertainment and we all felt sorry for him. I enjoyed jumping into the Square and back again through the empty window frame for the pleasure of boasting afterwards, 'Do you know, I've jumped right through that window. But I have. Truly.'

During Hitler's War I heard something go bang in the night, thought idly, 'That must be a bomb' and turned over in bed, thinking, 'And that's another one.' I was properly woken up by my sister, who came into the room carrying a glass of lemonade. She explained afterwards that she had picked this up from her bedside table instead of her torch, and we both thought it remarkable that in the circumstances she hadn't spilt a drop. She had only to say, 'Dad!' to have me awake and out of bed at a bound, for he had recently recovered from a severe heart attack, and we thought these bombs might well bring on another.

Downstairs in our parents' room it was all quite peaceful.

'What was that noise?' they asked sleepily.

'We think it was bombs,' said my sister.

'Where did they fall?'

'Must have been miles away or we'd all be dead by now,' I answered comfortably. I believed this, but an increasing disturbance outside drew me to the window and I could see flames rising from the army lorries parked on Church Green. People were milling about up there and I heard later that a Town Councillor, looking for the bomb craters, had found one by the time-honoured method of falling into it. Then our doorbell rang.

I ran down another flight of stairs to find our neighbour saying, 'Didn't you know your big window's gone?' I thanked him and hurried into the shop, expecting to see the entire stock and the carboys in smithereens, the goods in the window drenched in gallons of coloured water, and the place awash with medicines busily dispensing themselves. I could scarcely believe my eyes.

The three lovely carboys still stood serene, outlined against the sky; the blast had drawn out the window and dropped the fragments in a neat heap on the pavement. Inside, plenty of bottles were on the floor; they were quite unharmed, though the corks had popped out of three of them. Three, in all that multitude!

I emptied the window of goods, mopped up the contents of the uncorked bottles, and decided the rest could wait until morning. I found myself remembering the young officer with his swagger cane, but had no similar kindly feelings towards the young Nazi who, it was supposed, had found himself with a couple of unused bombs and simply thrown them out.

Our window was blocked with corrugated iron panels for a long time, and we had to work by electric light. Before the glass was replaced, I climbed through the frame into the Square for the sake of old times, but not quite as nimbly as before.

The shop changed little in appearance during the fifty three years it was run by my father and my sister. We all liked the old-fashioned mahogany counter, shelves, and display cupboards, and think our customers must have liked them too. The square mahogany drawers behind the counter were frequently admired, with their Latin names in black and gold under glass. At one time my favourite drawer was 'Cret:Gal:' because I knew what it meant and it contained lumps of chalk which I was allowed to have for marking out my hopscotch squares, though it was much too soft for the job and quickly wore away.

For the sake of their beauty we kept on the open shelves the old green ointment jars, dark blue syrup bottles, great tin canisters. They were there for years after we had ceased to keep them filled. Some of the glass shop-rounds with gold labels were still in use, but many were not. It would not have suited a time and motion enthusiast. A few years ago I saw a solution to this problem at the 'Apothecary to the Holy Ghost', an old chemist's shop in Vienna. Round the walls were open shelves filled with picturesque old jars, pots and bottles; packed goods for sale were on the counter, on stands or in cupboards, and the modern dispensary was out of sight, but the trouble was that it was almost too well arranged, like a stage setting. Ours, like Topsy, had 'just growed'.

In 1904 my father could take pride in the newness of the fittings; by 1957 my sister and I could be proud of their age and traditional appearance. At the halfway stage Father must have thought the shop needed a little bringing up to date, for he suddenly banished the tall, old-fashioned curved glass case on the counter and replaced it with two little flat modern ones. At once the shop looked completely wrong.

'I see fittings must be all new or all old,' Father declared, and out went the two modern cases. A learned doctor teaching at the Grammar School had them to display his scarabs, figurines and other Egyptian antiquities; our soaps and perfumes went back into the high curved case. My sister and I were so short that, when we worked in the shop, we peered over the top and really needed foot-stools, especially when commercial travellers came in for the first time, swept a dismissive glance over the pair of us and asked to see 'the pharmacist'. 'There she is,' I would reply, indicating my sister; the caller would pull himself together and, as likely as not, on his next visit come prepared with some nice little anecdotes, suitable for a female ear.

My father died halfway through the Second World War and it was through his death and the war itself that certain customs had to be dropped which he had first observed naturally and then taken care to preserve. Are there young people now who would instantly recognise that a play called *Pink String and Sealing Wax* must have something to do with a chemist's shop?

Father was quick and deft, and I have never seen anything like the speed with which he could wrap a piece of fine white paper round an eight ounce bottle, flick it into shape over the shoulders, put dabs of red sealing-wax to hold it top and bottom, and finish it off with a neat red seal over the cork. A piece of soap, probably wrapped already in two pieces of paper at the factory, would also have its white paper cover, be tied with thin red string, and even have a dab of sealing-wax to secure the knot.

During Hitler's War, paper was so scarce that shop-keepers were actually forbidden to wrap anything if it were not strictly necessary so, although we didn't have to send customers out clutching a loose handful of Epsom Salts, bottles and packets had to be taken away in all their nudity. Some people would sensibly bring their own paper and wrap the purchases up themselves, but it was amusing to see the horrified looks American soldiers gave us when they found they were expected to take unwrapped goods away. Unused to shortages, they thought this an uncivilised custom, protested vigorously, and could not see what the war had got to do with it.

Now when I take my own prescriptions to the pharmacy which is the grandchild of my father's, I find they nearly always ask for something he would have called a 'ready-made' or a 'reach-me-down'. The chemist who dispenses there tells me he has to make up only about ten per cent of the prescriptions he handles, as the modern tendency is towards pre-packaging. He showed me the dispensary, where I gazed at a small machine for dealing out tablets and a gadgetty typewriter for producing the labels. To me it was a revelation.

Nothing was being poured into measures, pounded in a mortar, boiled in a flask, filtered through a funnel, shaken in a bottle, or slapped on a marble slab. Everything was terribly tidy, the shelves stacked with neat packages instead of an assortment of jars and bottles, and the only relic I could see of the shop I knew was the large pair of polished brass counter scales set on a high shelf as an ornament.

Most of the prescriptions dispensed by my father and sister were for remedies individually made from a number of ingredients, so the tools of the chemist's craft were in constant use. These included sensitive small scales for powders and crystals, tapering glass measures for liquids, a marble slab and palette knife for ointments, pestles and mortars for pastes, a pill-board, and a compressor for slightly reducing the size of a cork to make it slip more happily into the bottle. The last time I saw one of these it was doing duty as a door-knocker. Pill-boards are probably museum pieces by now.

When I had grown tall enough for my eyes to be level with the top of the dispensing counter, I often watched in fascination the process of pill-making. A paste was first mixed and pounded in a mortar, then transferred to the pill-board which was made partly of wood, on which it was rolled, and partly of brass corrugations with sharp edges, on which it was cut. The roller, I thought, looked rather like a small pastry roller squashed flat; it was wooden one side and had brass corrugations on the other. The best part was seeing the paste rolled into a 'worm' between the wooden surfaces, then placed on the metal section to be cut by the corresponding part of the roller. This made the pills the right size but not the right shape, for they resembled tiny square cushions, very fat, and had to be rounded by being rolled on the board under what looked like a wooden jampot lid.

Pills were packed in circular boxes in many different sizes. The smallest held four. I was allowed to have a selection of boxes to turn into saucepans for my dolls' house. With a match-stick poked into the side for a handle, and a loop of stamp paper stuck on the lid, they gave me even more pleasure than those which could be bought at the penny bazaar.

It is a long time since I saw a cachet. These were small rice paper containers for powders, about the size of a shilling, and were supplied to the chemist in halves. The lower half was placed on a cachet board, in one of a dozen holes exactly the right size, then the correct weight of powder was slipped into the cachet through a tiny funnel. Next the top half was set in an ejector, had its rim moistened and was gently pressed onto the lower half. All this took a good deal of time, and the point of this kind of dispensing was that the cachet slipped down the throat easily and the container was quickly dissolved. Too quickly, I used to think, for I was sometimes given an empty one for myself as I loved the taste of rice paper, and tried to make it last with no success at all.

Other activities which I saw behind the dispensing screen were the boiling of sugar in a big pan for syrups, and of distilled water in glass flasks for eye-drops and lotions. Before it became customary to buy distilled water from a wholesaler, I used to see it falling slowly, drop by drop the whole day long, from a copper still. This was finally retired to the warehouse and sat there gathering cobwebs for years and years. No one disturbed the cobwebs, because inspectors of the Customs and Excise used to climb a ladder and examine the still from time to time, being troubled in their minds lest somebody should be secretly distilling illicit whisky.

Opening time used to be eight o'clock and closing time was not till seven — eight on Saturdays, and that last, tiring hour could be the busiest of the week. As Father had to spend so much time in the shop he thought he might as well enjoy it, and had vases of flowers and a tank of goldfish to brighten the scene, when these were so unusual that people used to comment on them. He was never more pleased than when a neighbour said to him, 'Do you know, I've been watching the customers leave your shop and they nearly all come out laughing?'

Outside there was a small arrowhead chipped into the kerb and pointing to our entrance. I first noticed this when I was a small child and took Father out to look at it.

'Oh yes, my dear, I knew it was there,' he said. 'I believe it's an old sign which some tramp has made to tell other chaps that ours is a good place to come to, and I'm very proud of it.'

Certainly, numerous tramps came in. Most of them asked for money or old clothes, but quite a few wanted some of the dried lavender flowers which were kept in one of our big stock bottles, and these they would offer for sale in tiny quantities contained in little envelopes or folds of paper, possibly so that they could defend themselves against the charge of begging. ·

Father pursued his hobbies — motoring, camping in tents or caravan, and photography — partly through discussions with people who came in to question him about them. In the early days of motoring it was quite a common thing for other enthusiasts to ask him for the best route to take to faraway places — towns as distant as fifty or more miles! — since Father adventurously explored roads and had a wonderful memory for such important features as potholed surfaces, bad hills, dangerous crossroads, and awkward corners. He could carry a map in his head and enjoyed sketching out routes for other people.

Much more serious problems were brought in, particularly up to some forty years ago, before everyone was covered by the National Health Service. A chemist's advice in case of illness was even more sought after then than it is now, and Father was constantly having to decide between suggesting a simple remedy himself and recommending the sufferer to consult a doctor. Many of his own recipes were well known and much sought after; years after his death we were still asked for them. I believe my sister was only defeated once when one of these was called for. In the fifties, an old man asked to be supplied with 'some of that stuff as your dear dad gin I as done I so much good when I as demobbed arter the 1914 war.'

As he couldn't tell us what trouble it was designed to cure, whether it was liquid, pills, tablets or ointment, whether it was swallowed, inhaled, or rubbed on the skin, we didn't stand much chance of success, though we did our best. Given a clue we might have found it in our records, which were ten years old when the 1914 war started.

In my time behind the counter I found that working out what customers really wanted could present interesting problems. Had the lady asked for Orlex or Horlicks? If we weren't perfectly sure, we would invariably offer the Malted Milk. Better to be thought deaf or dim than produce an unwanted hair colouring in the days when such things were kept a dark secret, and suggesting they might be wanted could be most offensive.

'Indecent tape' was easy, but so many people asked for it that we wondered what on earth our respectable adhesive dressing had done to deserve such a name.

I used to enjoy being asked for 'a tablet of B.O.' and handing out the soap extensively advertised to deal with that distressing condition.

One doesn't like appearing to be inquisitive by troubling customers with questions, but it was often advisable to ask them what they intended to do with the product. In this way we found a frightening number of people who proposed making lemonade from the attractively named but highly poisonous Salts of Lemon.

By a lucky chance my mind made the necessary leap so that I could deal with the lady who asked for Haddock Salts. She burst out laughing herself when I handed her a tin of Fynnon.

When a customer who often shopped for other people asked for a bottle of Cheese Linctus, she was shown a bottle of Gee's Linctus with a tentative, 'Is this the kind you want?' We were rewarded with a seraphic smile and the unexpected, triumphant comment, 'My friend said if I thought of Jesus I should remember it.'

Naturally there were awkward customers too, and I give the palm to a young American woman who wished to know if her photographs were ready but refused to give her name. Try as I would, I couldn't coax it out of her.

The conversation went something like this:

'Say, are my pikters ready?'

'What name, please?'

'The name doesn't matter.'

'I'm afraid I can't look for your photos if I don't know your name.'

'You don't say.'

'All photographs are filed alphabetically under customers' names. Won't you please tell me yours?'

'No.'

'Then if you don't mind waiting while I look at all the sets we have, I'll see if I can pick out yours.'

'Go right ahead.'

I went ahead. I went throught the entire batch of prints which were waiting to be called for. By great good fortune I could attach a face to all but two or three names. After looking through the prints in those packets and finding a set showing groups of American soldiers in uniform, I offered her that one, saying,

'I think these may be yours.'

'Sure.'

I couldn't see the point of her refusal but guessed I was being given some sort of a lesson. As one of our assistants always said of anything unexpected or untoward, 'It makes a change.'

A happier memory connected with photographs is of an elderly customer who brought us a negative showing him leaning on a five-barred gate. It was a most attractive snap and we weren't surprised that he wanted a re-print. There was a difficulty, though.

'Will you turn it over and print it t'other way round,' he said, 'so that it'll show me face.' Until then I'd thought that was a radio joke, but I don't think he was pulling our legs.

Displaced persons presented problems too. This was Second World War jargon for people who had been called refugees in the First World War. Many of those in our district were Poles, living in a hostel and working on the land. Their English might be rudimentary, but who were we to complain who hadn't a word of Polish? We did our best to understand them and wondered what they had had to put up with when they thanked us for not laughing. We certainly didn't laugh at them, but we did enjoy their visits.

Strangely, there were three products most frequently asked for by our Poles, their names all lending themselves to the long drawn-out vowels to which these customers were addicted. ''Ave you Zuuuuuuube?' they would ask, and we would happily hand the Zube Cough Mixture. To ''Ave you Zlooooone?' we would respond with a bottle of Sloan's Liniment while ''Ave you Zooooope?' was recognised as a request for soap.

Although I've had Poles asking for any two of these at once, I never had the hoped-for joy of hearing all three required at the same time. ''Ave you Zlooooone unt Zuuuuuube unt Zooooope?' would have made my day.

There was one Pole who wanted none of these things and we almost gave up in despair. The young man stood talking volubly and incomprehensibly, all the while dabbing his face in an agitated way. 'Simple' was our first thought as we produced soap, but it wasn't soap, and neither Zube nor Sloan's seemed appropriate. We offered in succession shaving cream, a shaving stick, and razor blades. The dabbing and torrent of words went on. We proceeded to face flannels and antiseptic ointment. No. Shaving Lotion, perhaps? Cold Cream? Mosquito repellent? Something for insect bites? All these goods were examined and rejected. Sunburn Lotion? An electric razor? With great good humour the young man went on making negative noises and dabbing his face with such vigour I thought that if he hadn't wanted a soothing lotion before he came in, he soon would.

Meanwhile other customers had arrived and our Pole drew aside so that we could serve them. He was probably glad of a rest. My new customer must have wanted some kind of surgical dressing because, as soon as I'd opened that particular drawer, there was an excited outburst of Polish in a different key while a hand appeared beside mine, seized a small packet of cotton wool and waved it joyfully in the air. Cotton wool! To dab on cuts when the razor slipped! To mop up what one of his compatriots, describing a fight at the hostel, had luridly called 'Bloods!' For two pins we would all have joined hands and played Ring-a-ring-of-roses.

To this day I enjoy hearing other people's reminiscences about our shop. In the butcher's only this morning an old customer told me how my father's name had cropped up in conversation at an Old Folk's Meeting and she had remembered how her husband and another boy used to race along to our shop immediately afternoon school was over. The first to arrive would ask if there was a bottle of medicine to be taken out, and if he was lucky he would deliver one and be given a ha'penny for his pains. This coin had possibilities in those days. 'Then he'd go along to Mrs Cooper's shop and buy a ha'porth of cold rice pudding from the big square slab which Mrs Cooper was always making, and she used to sell it in slices.'

That must have been before my time, as I can't remember when we had no regular errand boy until the supply failed at about the same time that Hitler's War ended. Once considered indispensable, these lads must by now be almost extinct. We had a rich variety working for us over the years and one of them, dating from my childhood, has passed into legend. I can vouch for the truth of these two incidents.

When he had been asked to fetch one of two boxes standing in the warehouse, the one required having been carefully described, this boy returned with the wrong box. Father, not at all surprised, merely said, 'Yes, well, please take this one back and bring the other one.'

'But Sir,' protested the lad, after a long pause for reflection, 'this is the other one.'

Another time he was asked to deliver a parcel at the other end of the town, dashed off immediately on the bicycle, arrived at the right house and rang the bell. 'I've come to bring you a parcel from the chemist,' he announced.

'Oh, thank you,' said our customer. Then, as nothing further was forthcoming, she added, 'Where is it?'

'They forgot to give it I,' he said.

Not all our boys were like that — far from it. One had demonstrated his magical powers by producing a cigarette from my sister's ear. My father had loved quoting the comment made by another lad after an immensely tall customer had left the shop: 'Coo! Ain't he up a depth?' and I had found particularly engaging the reply of a third, whom I'd asked if his grandmother was any better. 'Oh yes, thank you, quite better. She's fine! She could walk anywhere if it wasn't for her feet.' That had been followed not only by 'collapse of old party' but of the young one as well.

Sometimes it was a customer who rejoiced us with a slip of the tongue or unusual turn of phrase, such as the young mother who, bringing in a screaming baby to be weighed, asked us to excuse the noise as she'd just taken him to the Clinic to be humanised. We all thought that should be done more often. Another troubled person, with a wealth of gestures, described how badly her head 'hetched and herritated', adding that she had not washed her hair for thirty years but had kept it well oiled. In spite of its occurring in a sad setting, I couldn't help enjoying a third customer's quaint phrase about 'my poor dear husband as died three years ago come next Wednesday, all being well.'

Naturally into a chemist's shop comes plenty of suffering and sorrow, and before we left ours my sister had long worked through severe pain herself, not giving in until she could no longer stand without support, but that is not what I want to dwell on now. Behind our counter we had a great deal of fun and around it was, I think, a quality which only time can bring. My sister used to say 'Either we knew half our customers when they were in their prams or they knew us in ours,' and we'd been helped by assistants who had worked with us for nine, twenty, and thirty years.

When we had to say goodbye to it all, leaving the three great bottles to go on reflecting the life in the Market Square upside-down, it seemed to us that our lives had gone topsy-turvy too.

The Corn Exchange c1948, before it was abandoned and then restored. It lost its railings to a metal collection during the Second World War, but its balcony had not yet been condemned and removed. Mr A. H. Rowley's shop on the other side of the Corn Exchange Yard was bought by the Co-op in 1949 and the building replaced. The elm tree was killed by the Dutch Elm Disease and replaced by a young plane in 1980. (TW)

ABOVE: My grandparents, Mr and Mrs Alfred Leigh, on a drive to Newbridge, c1900. The Rose Inn became The Rose Revived in 1903. BELOW: Uncle Ted Leigh's Humber Light Car (1903), taken in 1908. The children are my cousins, Reggie and Rita Leigh, my sister Kathleen and myself. At the age of 17 Reggie joined the Royal Flying Corps, became a pilot, and was killed in France in 1918. (Both WTR)

The Wheels go Round

I was first wheeled out into the Square in a pram with high handles, like the shafts of a cart as there was no bar across to join them, and promoted from that to a pushchair in white painted wickerwork with a tall, straight back.

My next promotion was to a saddle fastened on the bar of my father's tall bicycle. There was a small footrest under the handlebars to support my feet. I felt safe there, between Father's arms, though the bicycle was like the pushchair and the pram, in having its seat much further from the ground than it would be today. On my seventh birthday I inherited my sister's small bike and she had a larger one.

Two on a bike used to be quite in order; it was even possible to take a lift on the back of a boy's. You put your foot on the mounting-step protruding from the centre of the back wheel, bent a knee on the carrier, and held on to the cyclist's shoulders. This couldn't be done on a girl's bicycle, as there was no mounting-step, necessary only on a high machine with a bar across the frame. By this means you could travel a mile or so reasonably well, but after that the step would cut into your foot, your other leg would be getting cramp, and it would be altogether more comfortable to get down and walk.

My mother and father used to sit on the seats of a bicycle made for two, but this was before my time and I met the tandem only in photographs.

Quite a few tricycles passed by, usually ridden by elderly people. Presumably this was because it wouldn't matter if the riders were no longer good at balancing, and if they needed a rest they could simply stop pedalling and sit still.

Horses drew most of the traffic that passed by my window and from time to time would cause great commotion by falling down. Those pulling great drays of the type used by brewers, coal merchants and the railway were most likely to fall because their loads were really heavy. It was difficult to get horses up again; they were frightened, their iron-shod hooves could get no purchase on ground slippery enough to have brought them down, the harness encumbered them and usually had to be taken off, and the excited crowd anxious to give advice got in the driver's way.

Loaded hay waggons were always a pleasant sight, but some of the most picturesque and exciting traffic to pass by came every September for the annual Fair. Except for their great size, the showmen's caravans and goods vans today do not look very different from other people's, but I used to watch horse-drawn caravans painted in bright colours with lace curtains at the little windows, which might have a chicken coop dangling underneath with the saucepans, and a dog running behind. Great waggons were piled with pieces of Fair equipment and the tarpaulins didn't completely cover everything. Poking out of the back of a van might be the polished brass rods, twisted like sticks of candy, which would presently bear the weight of the wooden horses and, with luck, my weight too. The sight of the gleaming brass was enough to make the blood tingle and the heart sing. Year after year my sister and I checked over the great names of the showmen's world as the heavy vans lumbered by. Were Studt's there with their galloping horses? What about Wilson's and Thurston's switchbacks? The helter skelter? The cakewalk? The joywheel? Then we would see the magic names, catch glimpses of those brass rods, of the motor cars from one switchback and the cat, the dragon, and cheeky dog with a cap on his head from the other, and know all was well. Look, there she was, the young woman with the darts! I saw her year after year until I realised she had become quite old and I wasn't so young myself, but at first, with a black apron over a long black skirt drawn tightly round a tiny waist, she represented for me all the vigorous show-women dressed in black who looked so quiet with their shopping baskets in the Square but cried their wares in such powerful voices on the Fairground. These voices could soften and become beguiling as you drew near and they urged you to risk your pennies and try your luck, among the deafening noise, the jostling, and the mingled smells of naptha flares and fish and chips.

The Fair gave us layer after layer of pleasure. We saw the waggons coming in, watched the roundabouts and swings being put together on the Fairground, went early to decide what we should like to see and do when Father could take us in the evening. After he had taken us home again — and we always had to leave early before the 'rough boys' came to thrust 'ticklers' in people's faces and throw violet powder and flour about — we would see the lights of the Fair from the windows and hear the roundabout organs bursting into their 'Hooo - hooo - hoooooo!' Finally there was retreating pleasure as we saw the vans and waggons pulling out. Goodbye to the hoop-las, the coconut shies, the stalls and booths, and the young woman with the tiny waist. Goodbye for another year.

The heaviest waggons were drawn by steam traction engines of the kind which are now rescued and lovingly restored. There is a special one which still appears in the Square when collecting for charity is afoot, and it is sometimes accompanied by a fairground organ. In the old days I didn't think much of them, whether they belonged to fair or farm, because they frightened my little dog, Brit. Either indoors or outside in the street, at the approach of one of these monsters, she would try to climb up me as if I were a tree, to be cuddled and comforted until whatever danger she had imagined had passed. My last dog behaved in the same way for helicopters but paid no attention to the noisiest plane.

For giving continual pleasure there was nothing like the traffic which passed through our own open gateway to explore the world. Father's bicycle gave way to a motorbike, and he soon had a sidecar attached to it so that he could take passengers. He could take them for miles — right out of the town to the surrounding villages — and like everyone else who drove a motor engine along the road, one of his first duties was not to frighten the horses, but slow down and crawl past them.

Our first sidecar was made of stout wickerwork, and looked exactly like the invalid carriages people used for pushing their grannies about. There was nothing to stop you falling out as there was nothing in front of you at all — not even the steering handle which all the old people held. You had to cling to the sides, and there was no more side to cling to than in an ordinary armchair.

Even these carriages represented progress, for they had started as trailers and had made their way from the back to the side because they had proved too tricky on corners. My father was fond of telling a story from *Punch* about a young motor cyclist who was pictured as half turning his head to call back, 'Look out, Auntie! There's another nasty corner coming!' Alas, it was too late. The trailer was empty. Auntie had already gone.

You knew about it more quickly if the passenger fell out from the side. I saw my father stop at once when my sister rolled out, quite gently, on to a grass verge, but he had hardly been moving and she climbed in again and wasn't even late for school.

By the time we had a new sidecar they were coach-built, provided protection for the feet and legs, and were so much built up at the sides that they had a little door. I was fascinated by this and spent most of its first morning opening and shutting the door, unfastening and fastening the catch, climbing in and out. It's a wonder the hinges weren't worn out long before Father had a chance to take it out of our yard and let its wheel turn on the road.

It was now quite difficult to fall out, so long journeys became possible and I travelled for a whole day sitting on Mother's lap. Poor Mother! It was the beginning of our annual pilgrimage by road to the relatives and beaches in Norfolk — quite an adventure since they were every inch of a hundred and eighty miles away.

'It can't possibly be done in less than twelve hours,' Father used to say. 'Start at six and we'll arrive at six. Start at eight and we'll arrive at eight.' We chose the earlier time and to this day, when I'm driving up to the relatives and beaches in Norfolk, I start at six o'clock in the morning.

Even then we weren't bumping along the road for the whole of that time. The twelve hours allowed pauses for picnic meals, poking about in the engine, and mending punctures. Especially mending punctures. Frightened or not, the horses got their own back by dropping nails from their shoes all over the roads for us to collect in our tyres. We did well to get through with only one puncture and our record was six. In my mind is a vivid picture of Father in his cumbersome motoring clothes, struggling with a wheel and a repair outfit while the rain poured down.

We were all exposed to wind and weather. On a fine day white dust billowed up from the unsurfaced roads so that each car travelled in a private cloud of its own making, keeping well behind the vehicle in front if there happened to be one, and avoided by anyone who chanced to be behind. Flocks of sheep and herds of cattle with dogs and drovers raised plenty of dust too so, children and all, we set out in light dustcoats to protect our clothes and with motor veils over our hats.

The veils held on my hat better than a piece of chewed elastic under the chin, and kept Mother's hair reasonably clean too, as she wore it in a bun on top of her head. Not even putting mine in pigtails stopped its feeling rough with dust when it was brushed out at the end of the journey.

I always thought it was Father who looked the most peculiar. Like other motor cyclists he wore his cloth cap back to front, and a huge pair of goggles. When it rained he put on a heavy waterproof jacket and stiff waterproof leggings, and looked as bulky as the Michelin Tyre man in the advertisements.

When friends waved you off from the Square and wished you a safe journey they weren't thinking of collisions, since there was so little traffic on the roads; they were thinking the engine might fail, and how right they were. Happily the few motorists about did not then regard one another as obstacles to be rushed past as quickly as possible but as fellow adventurers, so if anyone had stopped by the roadside they slowed down to find out why. Wave a sandwich or cup of tea at them and they'd be off again, but if the engine had given up they were ready with help and advice from their own experience, and if the petrol had given out they would produce some from their own spare can to help you on to the next place where petrol could be bought. These were few and far between; petrol pumps were well away in the future.

We drew up enquiringly too, and the most interesting thing we did was pull a motor cyclist out of a hedge. He had no idea how he came to be there but he and his machine were unharmed, so we

70

watched him set off again. People couldn't be given lifts when there was already one passenger in the sidecar, but when we had a car Father loved picking people up. Hitch-hikers hadn't invented themselves then, but he had a special fondness for the tramps who plodded along the roads, because they could spin such interesting yarns and there was no need to believe them.

Father enjoyed the joke against himself when he offered a lift to an old countryman who was apparently walking home from market. He replied with, 'Ah, I don't mind if I do,' climbed in for what was probably his first ride behind the engine and announced, 'I gets out 'ere,' almost before Father had changed into top gear. It must be the shortest lift on record.

Not everyone would trust himself to newfangled things for even that distance. There was a labourer who walked a good four miles to his work in the town every day, was never late and had never left early. One evening he was overtaken by a young apprentice on a motorbike who offered him a lift and was refused.

'Come on,' the young man urged. 'I'll get you home in five minutes and you'll be half an hour walking. Cock your leg over the back.'

He was so insistent that the labourer finally did as he was told and off the apprentice went. When he got off, no pillion rider was there, nor was he anywhere in sight. Much perturbed, the lad turned back to look for him, but he'd completely vanished.

Next morning the labourer was at work as usual and when he was asked what had happened explained. 'I cocked my leg over the thing same as you said, but let you drive off. I wasn't going to ride on that there contraption. When you come back, I hid in the ditch.'

I thought it was very grand to ride in our first motor car, but Mother surprised us all by saying she liked the sidecar better. 'It was more sporting,' she insisted but, goodness knows, just after the Kaiser's War, cars were quite sporting enough.

They did have sides and doors but not many had a roof. Rich people drove in limousines; we still sat exposed to wind and weather, still needing our dustcoats and motor veils. If it rained, we could stop and put up the hood. This wasn't done without serious consideration as it took some time and the sun might be out first. The hood lay along the back just like the one on a baby's pram, was pulled up, and had to be clipped onto the windscreen. Then there were four side-pieces to clip on too, and they were fiddley things. Not that we thought of them as a nuisance; to us they represented modern luxury, and they made our car more weatherproof than an uncle's had been. This could take three passengers, since it was a two-seater with a dickey at the back. The hood pulled up over the two front seats and I'd ridden in the open dickey crouching down under an umbrella.

71

Drivers didn't stop without good reason because it wasn't easy to get going again. They had to use a starting handle, and I used to watch them in the Square winding it round and round until it looked as if they were playing a barrel organ and a tune might break out at any minute. I listened with interest one teatime while my father and an uncle discussed a forecast made in a motoring magazine. 'Press a button and the engine starts itself! Whatever will they think of next, my boy?' I was used to hearing journeys described in great detail once we were home again, gear changes always being mentioned. 'Thought I'd do it in second but had to come down to bottom fifty yards from the top.' It was accepted that some hills were 'real stinkers', like Broadway and Birdlip, and that cars had to be coaxed up them.

Roadside repairs went on as they'd done with the motor bike. Father always seemed to be taking something out of the engine, poking at it with one of Mother's hairpins, blowing on it and putting it back. When bobbing and shingling came into fashion he begged all three of us to keep our hair long, for what would he do without hairpins? Other belongings were pressed into use. A seaside bucket was borrowed to fetch water from a stream to throw on the hubs of the back wheels. 'Overheated,' said Father darkly, making yet another journey with the little pail.

Children, dogs and chickens were other hindrances, making danger zones of most villages. Children — and chickens — really did play a terrifying game known as 'Last across the road'. Dogs rushed out barking hysterically at the wheels, children ran out with pencil and paper to collect the numbers on the numberplates. I hadn't many in my collection but I did know the registration letters of quite a few counties, and was excited whenever I saw an AH for Norfolk driving through the Square. I hoped that when Norfolk people saw our BW numberplates they would be equally impressed by our having come all the way from Oxfordshire.

My father became eloquent when he was hit in the face by a handful of gravel. Children often threw stones, probably for the same reason that the dogs barked — 'Here's something new, let's have a go at it.' How did we offend except by being new? The message squeezed out of the rubber bulb of our motor horn was not 'Get out of my way,' but 'Please look after yourselves.' Father once fixed a klaxon to the motor car when they had a brief vogue, but was afraid to use it in case the strident clamour should make somebody jump.

It was well before my time that the law required a man to walk in front of a motor car and carry a warning red flag, but there was in my childhood a well-known local character known as Joey the Flag, who was said to have borne this bright banner. At least, he should have done but insisted on waving a Union Jack instead. The first

72

speed limit I can remember is the more generous one of twenty miles an hour. When my father was teaching me to drive, one of his precepts was 'If the chap ahead of you is doing thirty miles an hour, my dear, don't attempt to pass him. Thirty miles an hour is fast enough for anybody.' Learning to drive at any speed satisfied me, for had I not once stood at the sitting-room window calling, 'Mother! Quick! Quick! Come and look! Here's a motor car with a lady driving it!' Mother came, at the double. She had never seen such a thing, either.

There were no driving schools or tests when I was learning. You bought a licence and learnt as you drove. One of my uncles drove for years, without accident, and without ever learning to reverse. If he took a wrong turning he just had to work his way round till he was facing the right way again. He always left the car in the same hotel yard in Norwich, where there was an obliging ostler who knew how to back it out. There was nothing in those days to stop him leaving it anywhere he chose in the streets, but Uncle was not one to leave a Model T Ford where it was in danger from children's sticky fingers. There was a great deal of brass about it, kept highly polished and in showroom condition. It's probable that Uncle spent more time cleaning it than driving it, and there is a legend in the family that every time the car stopped, my aunt would slip out and flick away the dust with a little feather brush.

Father also devoted a good deal of time to cleaning and polishing his car, checking it over before he went out, searching for the source of the tiniest squeak when he came back. Towards the end of his life, after he'd recovered from one of his heart attacks, the doctor told us he could go downstairs and do anything he felt well enough to do, but he must not stoop. We asked everyone to help prevent the stooping and I had a special word with the errand boy of the time ending with, 'If you can't manage to stop him yourself', do come and fetch me'.

The boy was splendid. A few days later his anxious face appeared in the shop's back doorway and he said, 'You'd better come at once. Mr Ransom's got his head below his numberplate.'

Father was one of the earliest trailer-caravanners and towed home his first van in the late twenties. The Other Chemist, who was also an East Anglian, strolled across the Square, stood gazing at the van, then said, 'Yew look like a dodman, bor.' Father was delighted. 'Dodman' is the Norfolk word for snail, the creature which takes its house about with it, so 'The Dodman' was adopted as the name of this caravan and of its successors.

The first 'Dodman', like the cars of the time, had never heard of streamlining, and looked like a small horsebox. It was a great novelty and everywhere we went people came along to stare. Of course there were no recognised caravan sites; we asked permission every time we wanted to stop for a night or longer, usually on a farm. The number of people who wanted to ask questions, or explore the van's ingenious interior, could be a nuisance, but I remember with affection an old countryman who leaned on a gate and watched us closely for half an hour or so before calling out:

'What time does the show start?'

'Oh, there isn't a show. Sorry, we're not giving a show.'

'What be you a'selling, then?'

'Oh, sorry, we don't sell anything.'

'Whatever be you a'doing of it for, then?'

He was too polite to comment when we said we did it for fun, but his face told us plainly he thought that was a funny sort of fun, that was.

Not until Hitler's War was over did I have a car of my own. It was one which had already been cherished for over ten years and it was cherished for almost another twenty by me. By the time I reluctantly parted with it, not only did I love it but have the quite irrational feeling that it loved me and I was letting it down.

When it first arrived, sound in wind and limb, my sister was moved to say, 'Well, if 'er ent bent yet, 'er soon 'ull be,' and the little Morris 8 of the vintage year 1935 was known as the Bentley from that day on. Once when I was strolling round Cirencester I heard a young man call out to a young woman, 'The Rolls is just round the corner!' and was sufficiently interested to slip round and see what sort of a Morris-Bentley their car was. Round the corner was a real Rolls and it had a uniformed chauffeur in attendance. It made my day.

The speed at which the Bentley liked to travel was twenty-seven miles an hour, but I could persuade it to do thirty-five without feeling I was asking too much and we tucked right into the side of the road as we knew our place. My sister used to say it made her feel giddy to see the prams whizzing past. It stands to reason I couldn't pass anything much faster than a bicycle or tractor but that suited me very well. I was impressed with the way other drivers took care of me. They gave me plenty of room and I didn't need much; they would draw into a layby and wave me on when I had been following them happily for miles, and one lorry-driver even stopped to make sure I was all right when the Bentley and I were resting in a layby ourselves and she was cooling off with her bonnet up. This, at least, was a piece of old time chivalry that made me feel I ought to have a sandwich to wave at him and that, if I turned to look, I should find a bucket and spade on the back seat. Now I am driving a perfectly ordinary-looking car I have to look after myself; I noticed the difference immediately.

Now motoring can be more of a penance than a pleasure, I like to remember the funny sort of fun it used to be. I'm glad to have been on the roads when there were no road licences, MOT Certificates or

74

Highway Codes; no white and yellow lines, traffic lights, one-way streets and roundabouts; no pedestrian crossings, dual carriageways and motorways, and no No Parking. I like to remember the people driving traps, governess carts and hay waggons, who forbore to scowl if you'd managed to crawl past them without frightening the horses, and the earliest AA men who saluted you, with a smile, if your car wore their badge on her bonnet.

When we left the Square, it was in a little old Bentley that I drove through our gateway for the last time. I had only Mother on board as my sister had already gone in an ambulance. Mother had stayed indoors for so long that she was protesting I was driving too fast while I was still in second gear, and had not yet reached Church Green.

Cars can no longer be driven through my part of the Square, nor can they be harboured there in strictly marshalled rows, but it has been pressed under plenty of turning wheels in its time, ours amongst them, from the days when anyone trusting himself to a horseless carriage set out on an adventure and returned with a tale to tell.

My mother, sister and an Edwardian pram in sunshine in our garden (1904), which is now under concrete in Woolgate. (WTR)

ABOVE: A chairload of cousins — two Knights, Philip and Charles — between two Ransoms, c1911. LEFT: Mother claimed to be the first woman in Witney to own a bicycle. RIGHT: The children's first bicycle was no little toy. This was a Raleigh, about 1909. (All WTR)

RIGHT: Father's first sidecar. Like an invalid's Bath chair, it was made of wickerwork, which the snapped-on waterproof apron almost conceals; 1910. LEFT: Our first sidecar with a door. Mother and I are wearing motor-veils and I have goggles too, c1911. CENTRE: My sister and I have dressed up as Mother and Father, and are ready to go, c1912. (All WTR)

BELOW: When there was so little traffic on the roads, parties of motorcyclists would go out together. Here are Mr and Mrs Valentine (tailor), Mr and Mrs Buckingham (jeweller) and my mother, perched up in the wickerwork sidecar at the back with Rex Valentine sitting on Father's saddle. When Rex left school he was apprenticed to my father and became a qualified chemist. (WTR)

ABOVE: Another example of Leigh and Sons' modernisation — in 1917 they had a mechanically propelled vehicle, and the load looks as if it was held together by faith and hope. (IL) BELOW: Father's first car, an Overland 1920. The hood is folded back like one on a baby's pram. (PR)

ABOVE: 'The Dodman', Father's first caravan, 1929. BELOW: A picnic on the long, adventurous road to Norfolk, c1913 — we have not taken off our dust-coats and motor-veils. (Both WTR)

ABOVE: I used to run down The Hill to Hillside School, here almost obscured by trees at the bottom. The building jutting out is the Old Post Office, No 1 High Street. (PR) BELOW: An early photograph of Hillside School, usually called 'Miss Walker's'. The entrance for pupils was down the yard to the left. It is now a part of the West Oxfordshire Technical College; the house on the right, now the Post Office, used to be the doctor's home and surgery. (TW)

A Square Education

To my right, obscured from my window by the block of buildings where the Other Chemist was to be found, stood the doctors' surgery in a handsome house which is now our handsome Post Office. It was there, as a grown-up, that I heard two pronouncements about my health which I didn't find helpful at the time but are a source of joy now.

Feeling I could no longer put up with some recurring symptoms, I described them to a doctor and asked if anything could be done.

'How long have you been like this?' he asked.

I made a rapid calculation. 'The first attack I can remember was at least a dozen years ago.'

His face cleared. 'Oh well,' he said comfortably, 'it can't be anything serious or you'd be dead by now.' That was that.

Not wanting to be caught that way again I went along some months later to consult him about a new trouble.

'How long has this been going on?' I was asked.

I had my answer ready. 'About ten days.'

'Oh well, you must give it a chance to clear up by itself.'

You can't win, but I'm still here and the doctor was a character whom the town loves to remember.

It was often worth the time spent in the waiting-room to hear the fascinating conversations that went on down there; one I particularly remember, though it took place many years ago, was between two Senior Citizens speaking very slowly and taking long pauses for reflection. It was not about ailments, as one might expect, but about the recent raising of the school leaving age.

'It stands to reason they can't learn them nothing, once they've turned fourteen.'

'And it's a lot of rubbish — all that stuff about old kings and that. And as for geography!'

'I left when I was thirteen and I reckon I had a good education, I did. Our Gaffer at St Mary's was the best Gaffer there was.'

'No, I reckon my Gaffer at Cogges was thought to be the best. He was a real schoolmaster. My, how he used to wallop 'em! Yes, out came the stick for any little thing. He was a real schoolmaster, Gaffer Fallows was.'

'And they learnt them religion better in them days, too. Every morning we had it. Religion. Four curates there was in them days and every morning we had religion from a real clergyman.'

By those standards my education was poor indeed. No stick and no real clergymen, but plenty of old kings and I loved meeting them.

My school was in a big house next door to the surgery, and I could walk along either side of the Other Chemist's block to reach it. There was a choice between adventurously crossing the great width of the Market Square to gain the pavement, after a satisfying climb up four stone steps, or walking past a minor hell of flames before crossing the road.

This was an inferno of fire, sparks, stamping, hissing, and the clanging of iron. I didn't linger there if the smith was shoeing a horse, but clenched my fists and ran past. I knew it would hurt me to have hot iron nailed to my palms and the soles of my feet and I was sure it hurt the horses too, though they stood there quietly enough. I did love looking at the great cart-horses with their hairy ankles as they waited their turn, tied to the iron ring in the wall outside the forge. The ring outlived the smithy by many years but has gone now, and the optician doesn't need it.

When I joined this school at the ripe age of five I was no novice, having spent the previous summer term being broken in at another one in a big house on the Green, probably chosen because it was on our side of the road. It closed at the end of my first term and my sister teased me for being its last straw. 'One term of you and they gave in,' she said for ever after.

I must say that they didn't seem to know what to do with me when I was there. From their point of view I must have been a great nuisance, since I was by far the youngest pupil and had turned up late in the school year.

I used to arrive in my wickerwork pushchair and was taken into the kitchen, where someone I thought of as 'the old lady in black who doesn't teach' — she was actually the owner of the school — took off my coat and bonnet before sitting me on the table to change my shoes. Goodness knows why she had to do that, since they had only touched the ground when I left the pushchair to walk in at the front door. My sister went to the cloakroom and took off her outdoor things for herself.

On the first morning I can have been neither frightened nor unhappy, because I whistled. The two ladies in the room couldn't have enjoyed this very much — it was a recent accomplishment and I was still experimenting — because a bigger girl was told to sit by me and keep me quiet. I liked that, for she was my cousin.

From that moment I became the buck that everybody passed. No activity seemed to have a place for me in it so I was chiefly cast in the role of observer. I sat on a Big Girl's lap in the playground and fingered her watch while the other pupils were having drill. Wrist watches were then a novelty and hers was exactly like the little ones ladies wore pinned to their blouses, or tucked into their waistbelts at the end of a long chain, except that it was held inside a clumsy leather case strapped to the wrist. Later my sister had one just like it. The playground was a pleasant place to sit in because it was more like a garden, and there were birds and butterflies and flowers to look at, besides the watch and the rows of girls and boys marching round and round or swinging their arms about.

I don't know if the ladies had ever heard me sing; perhaps the whistle was enough to persuade them they had better not let me try. I had to sit and listen while the others chirruped away round the piano. There was plenty to look at in the classroom as there were charts on the walls which showed all kind of butterflies and flowers, but I liked the outside ones better. I have a faint memory of being given some crayons or plasticene to play with now and then.

I don't remember anyone giving me reading lessons, but I do remember sitting at a little table with one of the ladies and two or three children who read aloud in turn. I listened, looking at the print and the pictures. The book was called *The Peep of Day*. When the school closed and each one of us was given something to take home for a souvenir, a copy of this book was given to me and I still have it. Between its pages are preserved some of my treasures — pressed flowers and leaves, with a surprising number of four-leaved clovers, and bits of silver paper, all lovingly put there when I could read the print for myself.

It is a quaint little book. A publication of the Religious Tract Society, it is described on the frontispiece as 'a series of the Earliest Religious Instruction the infant mind is Capable of Receiving'.

In the first seven chapters my infant mind was instructed about the body — today it seems necessary to stress that there was no mention of sex — in a mother's care, the soul, good and bad angels, and the world. Three chapters were devoted to the world. Then Adam and Eve and The First Sin each had a chapter and the remaining forty-one told the story of the New Testament. The pictures showed children picking flowers, sleeping, praying, being cuddled, and gathering round Jesus. There were also shown a few familiar creatures — a dog, a cat, a fly, and some chickens — to represent the animals of the world. These have no souls, my infant mind was assured.

The whole text can be summarised as 'God's in his heaven, all's right with the world', with the words 'if you are good' added in a firm voice.

My recollections of it are not all happy. I remember enjoying the pictures, getting impatient with the halting voices of the other children because this wasn't reading aloud as I knew it at home, and feeling sick when one of them stumbled over the words 'they put nails in His hands and His feet, so they nailed Him to the cross'. I clenched my hands, just as I did later when passing the forge. Of course it hurt Him. I knew, for I'd driven a sewing-machine needle through my finger when giving an enquiring turn to the handle, and that wasn't as big as a nail. Years later I felt sick at this moment in the theatre at Oberammergau where the nailing to the cross was dealt with realistically, but at least didn't have to be carried out through the audience with a number of other people.

Someone somewhere must have taught me how to make figures and count up to twelve. Arithmetic lessons always began with our writing out as many of the multiplication tables as we knew, and this was an occasion when I was given a slate and a squeaky pencil with the rest. Often sitting in the garden-playground on a wooden stump with a bench for a table, I laboriously set out the pattern I saw the other children making. It was nothing but a pattern to me and went something like this:

$$2 \times 1 = \quad ; 2 \times 2 = \quad ; 2 \times 3 = \quad ; 2 \times 4 = \quad .$$

and so on. I might get three or four tables written out this way before it was time to stop. I didn't put anything after the equals sign as I had no idea what to put, and nobody seemed to mind so it couldn't have mattered. I was perfectly happy; for once I had been taken out of the stalls and was in the thick of the action on the stage.

This was the scholastic education I took to my next school. Whatever its failings I had been well trained in the arts of sitting still, looking on, and tackling anything that did come my way.

My new school was run by three ladies, all sisters. During my seven years' attendance there two left to have weddings, and were replaced by younger members of the family, while a still younger sister was a pupil with me. When I first went there, the girls in the top form had long skirts and their pigtails were rolled up and pinned to their heads, but by the time I left the age of the top class was about twelve and I was in it.

My time for sitting down and looking on had come to an end. The sisters kept me busy and I liked it. I knew the letters of the alphabet because they were on my building bricks; I knew the order they came in because we chanted through the alphabet again and again in a singing-game we played at parties. Quite soon the sisters had attached them to sounds and I was making my halting way through various readers. The excitement of reading came when I picked up a book belonging to my sister and called *Tom and Maggie Tulliver,* which must be one of the most tantalising books ever printed for children. It reproduces the childhood scenes from *The Mill on the Floss* without any explanation or continuity; having aroused interest it simply stops, so you never know what happened to the rebellious Maggie and her brother Tom, however many times you read it, however hard you try to find out. My big excitement came on the very first page when Mr Tulliver delivered his pronouncement about Tom's future: 'I mean to put him to a downright good school next Midsummer.'

I sat staring at this line. 'Downright,' I was thinking. 'Downright.' That's a hard word and I'm reading it. I can read. I can read!' That was the moment I turned into a bookworm.

Writing was developed in Copy Books, with model writing to copy. These books had double lines and you wrote between them, first letters, then words, then phrases, and finally proverbs and other short sentences which stretched across two wide pages. At first I didn't like having to write with a pencil while everyone else had a pen and ink. I went through a period which must have tried the patience of whichever sister was in charge, when I dabbed my pencil noisily on the table every time the girl opposite dipped her pen in the inkwell. Eventually I was given a penholder with a steel nib and dabbed away to some purpose. From that moment my middle finger was smothered in ink to the second knuckle, and it stayed like that for about thirty years until ballpoints came in and I cleaned it up for good.

I also learnt how to fill in the missing figures from the multiplication tables and to understand what they meant, which was quite a revelation. Though I still have to work out seven times eight and twelve times seven because those answers didn't stick, I have found the tables useful knowledge and I hope the authorities who have dropped them from the curriculum know what they are doing.

There was one piece of apparatus for helping us with our sums which was both simple and effective. It was nothing but the tops of the tables at which we sat in small groups. The surface was marked out in squares an inch wide, so if you wanted to be quite sure that $12 - 5 = 7$ you had only to count twelve squares, cover five of them up and count the remainder, to have your confidence restored. Recently I asked two former schoolmates if they had brought away some special memory from the school and was surprised by their answers. 'Oh yes,' each one said. 'The little squares on the table tops.'

We had exercise books with the pages marked in squares for arithmetic homework so were not too badly handicapped when sitting at our own more ordinary tables. For some years we still used slates in class, and there can be no more satisfactory way of wiping out one's errors than with a damp sponge, however much it smells. The disappearance of the mistake is total and final.

The exercise books with squares were used in our first drawing lessons, too. On cards rather bigger than postcards, covered with similar squares, were pictured objects as varied as a policeman or a sprig of holly. All the lines were straight — horizontal, vertical and diagonal — and we reproduced the pictures faithfully in our exercise books by counting the squares. I could produce something quite recognisable by this method, but it didn't give me a clue how to cope with the freehand designs or sketches of animals which were given us to copy later, still less how to deal with the still-life groups comprising such objects as a watering-can and a flowerpot with an improbable piece of drapery, round which we sat in hopeful circles at my Grammar School.

We started French at about the age of eight and really did use that little pink book called *French Without Tears* of which the aunt with the pen is now considered to be the heroine. I was more interested in Robert and Georges. One was big and one was little and the big one had a penknife which he would not lend. Unfortunately, when some small Belgian refugees joined us during the Kaiser's War, we found it difficult to confine conversation to pens and penknives and were quite at a loss. Later, one of our pleasures came from learning a particular list of words which were 'exceptions to a rule'. 'Bijou, caillou, chou, genou, hibou, joujou, pou', we used to chant, ending with a giggle and a pounce on 'pou'. 'Louse' might be a forbidden word in English, but it could be spoken lawfully in French and we made the most of it.

It was all the lessons which came under the heading of English which held my complete allegiance. Grammar, with its parsing and analysis, had the same sort of fascination for me as a jigsaw puzzle and I can't think why it has become a dirty word. Composition was easy since it called chiefly for a good memory, and I had one. It usually consisted of listening twice to an anecdote or piece of description , then reproducing it in words as near as possible to the original.

The poetry offered to us had rhymes you could hear and a rhythm you could feel, and I loved it. The preference was for narrative verse and we did a great deal of learning by heart. My head held for years all *The Revenge,* most of *Horatius* and long passages from *Marmion* and *The Lay of the Last Minstrel,* with many ballads which went in at my eyes and came out at my mouth almost as easily as a disc turns on a turntable. Mine was a photographic memory which the rhyme and rhythm helped.

When I went away to school, the English mistress didn't believe me when I said I had not read *Julius Caesar* before, but I hadn't. What I had done was sit on the pigsty wall on long hot afternoons hearing my sister recite famous passages from the play until I could prompt her without the book. She was preparing for an exam. I was too shy to tell the rather stiff English mistress about this, though the pigsty hadn't had a pig in it for years.

'English' was also Shakespeare, which was poetry too, and by the age of eleven I'd become an addict. I had read and re-read the now despised *Lamb's Tales,* which told the stories so clearly that I was free to enjoy the way the plots unfolded when I met the real play. I'm always a little sad when people say they hate Shakespeare because they 'did' him at school, since that was where I learnt to love him.

As You Like It was my first real taste of Shakespeare and it seemed very like the stories in fairy tale books, except for being told in more interesting language. The sentences that didn't make sense here and there could be skipped. When we reached the stage of 'acting Shakespeare' at the end of term, we had no platform, curtain, scenery, or costumes, and no audience other than the sisters and the rest of the small school sitting in the biggest classroom, where the desks had been folded up and leaned against the wall.

The older girls presented the Trial Scene from *A Merchant of Venice*. Shylock, in a white blouse and navy skirt, looked quite frightened as she threw up a stiff arm and a clutched knife and said bleakly, 'A sentence! Come, prepare!' My class followed with the Banishment Scene from *As You Like It*, and this was one of the occasions when that good memory of mine got me into trouble. There can have been no other reason than this memory for choosing someone so undersized to play Rosalind, so there I was, conscious of my smallness through constant teasing and having to drink vast quantities of cod liver oil, enquiring:

'Were it not better
Because that I am more than common tall,
That I did suit me all points like a man?'

The house was too well trained to be brought down by this suggestion, but there was silent laughter on everybody's face.

I was pleased to meet Shakespeare again in the history book. History was learned by the method of reading a book and becoming familiar with its contents. After a rather half-hearted drifting round with the Romans, the Anglo Saxons, and the Danes, the book led us onto firmer ground, where Alfred built the navy and possibly burnt some cakes, and Edward the Confessor built Westminster Abbey. Then proper history began with William the Conqueror and was divided squarely into reigns. These all fascinated me until we came to Queen Anne's, when everything became less romantic and more political, but we plodded on to finish in the reign of Queen Victoria. Whether we never got to the end of the book before the end of term, or whether the author finished writing it before Queen Victoria died, I can't say, but my recollections end with some sort of trouble with a potentate I still think of as King Coffee of Ashan Tea.

There were junior and senior editions of this book and we went through the junior one several times before being promoted to the next, so that the pair of them lasted me until I left the school. There was more detail in the senior book and so it was fatter, and I was glad to be promoted to it because I'd liked it when I'd borrowed it from my sister. What particularly attracted me was the addition of footnotes, though they were in lamentably small print, for among them were quotations from Shakespeare's historical plays. It really did make you see how horrid Henry VIII had been when you read the words the play put into the mouth of Katharine of Aragon.

Other countries didn't appear to have much history and were a poor lot. We heard of them from time to time, when we had to wage war with them, and beat them though out-numbered, or when a Dutch Admiral sailed the English Channel with a broom at his masthead, which was very impertinent of him. However, other countries did have geography, and they had shapes.

We spent quite a lot of time looking at maps. I loved them. Father used to pore over maps of England and Wales, thinking where it would be nice to go, and I liked maps of other countries which I hoped to visit one day. I don't remember having any lessons which explained maps to us; we were shown a shape in a book, told which country it represented, and took it in our stride. We did copy maps into special exercise books, first pencilling an outline and then inking it over with a specially fine nib.

Geography seemed to concern itself chiefly with the British Isles and with products like coal and wool. There were lists to be learned of bits of land that stuck out into the sea, and of bits of sea that washed into the land, and I think these gave me my passion for standing on extreme tips, from Portland Bill to North Cape.

I do remember being so fascinated by the building of the Canadian Pacific Railway that I resolved to cross Canada on it and did, though not until half a century had passed.

Scripture was taken at first by a retired teacher who loved the school too well to leave it. She was one of the sisters who had owned the school before my set of sisters took it over, and she had a most fascinating handbag. We all stared at it. It was made of fur with an extra piece sewn across the back so that it was a muff as well. This lady didn't sit at the desk but on a separate chair, so we could see how she liked to keep her hands in the muff on her lap. She told us stories from the New Testament and always ended the lesson by giving us a sentence from the Bible to remember till next week. This didn't require a great effort, especially when it was as short as 'Jesus stood still' or 'Jesus wept'.

The new lesson always began by our being asked who could remember last week's text, and that good memory brought me trouble yet again. My hand always went up, and one morning I was astonished when a most reproving glance came my way. 'How can you remember it when you were not here?' the lady asked. I was bewildered. 'I do remember it,' I insisted. 'Then please say it,' came the cold instruction. I obeyed and the atmosphere cleared.

'You have remembered the text from the week before and forgotten about being absent,' said the lady, much mollified. Another child was asked for the text required and so everybody's honour was saved.

After Miss Early stopped coming, the sisters took over her lessons and I remember being embarrassed myself when a sister turned pink. 'Please Miss Gladys, what is a wum?' asked the boy sitting next to me. 'There's no such word,' said the sister, and I saw her colour rise. 'Oh yes there is,' said the boy, firmly but politely, frantically turning over the pages of his Bible in an effort to come across it. Then I suddenly realised which word he was looking for; I knew how to pronounce it though I had no idea what it meant, and I was pretty sure it came under the heading of things not spoken about, so I punched him. Turning a hurt and indignant look on me he saw the face I was pulling, and sat down. The lesson went on as if no question had been asked and that was the end of the matter.

The other sister went pink on what I hope for her was a happier occasion, and it was certainly nothing to do with Scripture. She had glorious red hair, the kind that springs up with a life of its own. Restless under the intent gaze of another of my classmates she asked, 'Why are you staring at me?' and received the perfectly straight and truthful answer, 'Please Miss Winifred, I was thinking how lovely your hair looks with the sun shining on it.'

We had drill in the playground when possible and stood in line, stretching our arms this way and that, bending our knees outward till we almost sat on the ground, or keeping them straight while we tried to touch our toes. We marched round and round, up the middle, one to the left, one to the right, joining again, left right, left right; it was all great fun.

The playground was unusual since it was on two levels. At street level was a small yard paved with blue-grey pieces little bigger than bricks, impressed with diagonal lines which were an obstacle for even the best spinners of tops. Some half dozen steps led up to the main playground, which still looked rather like a garden. There was a greenhouse with junk in it, remnants of flower borders along the sides and traces of a lawn in the well-trodden centre where we drilled and played. There were a few bushes and a big chestnut tree which encouraged us to turn up early in the conker season to take our pick. We even gathered up the tiny ones, little bigger than peas in their spiky cases, and threaded them up for necklaces. Though I loved the glossy brown chestnuts in their soft, lined beds of cream and green, I was not behindhand in piercing them ruthlessly and stringing them up for the fierce conker contests.

Here we played the usual games as their seasons came round, such as skipping, hopscotch and marbles. There was not enough room for bowling hoops, and I think the most popular game was tag, in all its varieties. In all running and chasing games, the word we shouted for a brief truce was 'cree', which I believe was unknown outside Oxfordshire.

We strictly observed the two anniversaries of April Fools' Day and Shickshack Day. On 1 April we were busy making fools of as many people as possible before noon; on 29 May we wore oak leaves in memory of Charles II and his sheltering oak tree. There was a rhyming couplet to remind us:

'Twenty-ninth of May,
Shickshack Day,'
and we went round chanting it. When I went away to school no one had heard of either 'Shickshack' or 'cree' and I am quite unable to account for them now. I wonder how many people today observe Oakapple Day under any name.

During the 1914 War we went mad about aeroplanes, and the craze lasted us for one whole summer term. Planes were then a novelty which brought people running out of their houses to look up at the sky, and we happily showed off if we could tell an Avro from a Sopwith or a Bristol Fighter.

We made toy planes for ourselves and very crude they were — we never dreamed of making scale models, still less ones which could fly, but were content to put together a plaything in the general shape of an aeroplane, using any materials which came to hand. Chiefly we saw biplanes, and I found the two pieces of wood from a date box just right for wings when I'd smoothed the roughness away. A flat piece of wood at right angles to them, a triangular bit sticking up for a tail, and there you were. I think no one attempted wheels, but we did want propellers, and were fortunate in having among us a boy with the knack of carving them out of scraps of wood; he was kept busy supplying the less gifted. They revolved on pins pushed into the front of our aircraft if we blew hard enough but, as too much blowing made us giddy, we spent most of playtime rushing round to make the propellers whirl on the planes held high above our heads.

No two were alike and what distinguished mine was having a pilot. I had a little china doll, not more than one and a half inches high, with movable arms and legs, and I contrived a uniform into which he could be sewn, by knitting khaki darning wool on two of Mother's hairpins. I even managed a forage cap. Those were the days of the Royal Flying Corps, before aviators had become the boys in blue of the RAF. To ensure the safety of my pilot I sat him on a spot of seccotine, and I stuck his cap on too as I hadn't thought of a helmet.

At one time we contrived an aerodrome by cutting off a corner of the playground with walls of earth about two inches high, and arranging our planes inside this, ready to take off. A take-off was simple — each owner swooped on his plane and ran off with it. Authority tolerated the airfield until we had the bright idea of defending it from Germans by sticking pieces of broken glass along the walls, and then came down on the side of the enemy by having the whole thing swept away.

A year after the war ended I went away to join my sister as a boarder in a Grammar School, with my head full of Angela Brazil and midnight feasts in the dorm. The first thing I had to do there was adapt myself to the more sophisticated playground fashion of walking round and round with a chum.

How old-fashioned all this is now; the simple, home-made playthings, the lessons depending on methods now despised — learning by heart, copying models — but these methods can produce results and put firm ground under the feet of those taking off on imaginative flights.

When I was training as a teacher, something called the Play Way was being advocated; learning was to be less formal, more pleasant and more effortless; imagination was to be preferred to memory. It sounded wonderful then, but it has led to a Never Never Land full of shapeless mists where direction posts have crumbled into decay and children been left to flounder.

Twenty years after I had given up teaching and not long after we had left the shop, I found myself back in the Square, working part-time in the house with the steps which had been given away to benefit children. I was engaged in the further education of teenagers whose nearer education had not, in many cases, gone far enough, and trying to explain why such forms as 'We was' will not do in commercial correspondence. This had to be done without the use of the simplest grammatical terms since the students didn't know any. I decided it would save time if they became acquainted with a few elementary ones, and the iron curtain came down at once.

'We don't have to know that sort of thing now,' they said with metaphorically tossed heads, and defended all their errors with 'It sounds all right to me' and 'You know what I mean'. I thought they had a right to be told the basic rules of their own language; anyone would have known what they meant when they shot a ball between the posts on a hockey or soccer field, but a declaration of 'offside' wouldn't be much use to them if no one had ever explained the rules.

It puzzled me that they made such heavy weather of looking up words in a dictionary until I realised that many of them didn't know the alphabet. What possible harm can there be in teaching it, and how can people deprived of it deal with a telephone directory, even if they never need to meet a filing cabinet?

OVERLEAF: After going up The Hill, one passes the Marlborough Hotel (right), the Town Hall and Buttercross (left) and eventually arrives at Church Green. (TW) ABOVE: Witney's first batch of volunteers to enlist in the Army is marching up The Hill on its way to the Station, passing Cook and Boggis's Department Store and Jackson's Forge (far right), 1914. (TW) BELOW: It's a Long Way to Tipperary. (WTR)

The Kaiser's War

In August 1914 we were in the kitchen behind our shop when my sister spread the newspaper on the table and set about making me understand what was happening in the world outside.

'This big country,' she said, dabbing at a map of Europe, 'is going to fight this little one.'

Her fingers were pointing to the two countries whose quarrel exploded into the First World War — sprawling Austria-Hungary and compact little Serbia.

I gathered that other countries had started to pick sides as if they were playing Oranges and Lemons or Nuts in May. People were saying we might have to join in and, if we did, it would be on the smaller country's side, which seemed only fair to me.

Someone had started it all off by shooting an Archduke. Well, people like that were always fighting in fairy tales and it always ended happily before the book was closed. This quarrel went on in a most bewildering way long after the newspaper had been folded up.

The trouble had already brought us back early from a seaside holiday in Norfolk, in case the soldiers wanted to use all the trains, and you had to believe something was going on when the Square became full of khaki uniforms marching about and forming fours. The khaki columns still live in my memory as a background for some unforgettable moving pictures.

The first series is an inspection of the local Volunteers in whom I took a special interest because my father was one of them. He had been scornfully turned down by the doctors who decided whether you could join the Army or not; they had sent him home with a shilling and a piece of paper to say he was totally unfit for military service, so he joined Dad's Army. At that time these soldiers were known as Volunteers.

First he was given a scarlet armband with a crown and the letters GR on it in black, then a khaki jacket, and later still a pair of corporal's stripes. If a peaked cap and perhaps khaki trousers joined this outfit I believe that was the extent of it, for on volunteering he had stipulated that he should not be asked to drill or to march. Most people might think that this would limit his usefulness as a soldier, but Father had won a rifle-shooting contest and it was probably thought he might fire a shot or two if the war came so near he didn't have to march away and look for it.

What he did was office work, which he always referred to ambiguously as 'keeping a list of the mugs', and he helped look after the Leafield Poles. These curious new poles we had been gazing at surprisingly turned out to be of national importance, and we were all proud to be living near them when it was whispered that they had intercepted a secret German message. The Germans were expected to have a go at them at once, so the Volunteers had to take it in turn to guard them every night. My father enjoyed this duty and usually returned home as happy as a lark when morning came. He said the best part was cooking his breakfast in a frying-pan over a little picnic stove which spluttered so much that everybody called it Lloyd George.

My sister and I were equally happy to find that the Germans hadn't shot him in the night, and used to greet him by bawling a song which might well have been in the top ten if anyone had bothered to work it out in those far-off days.

'Now poor Father's joined the Witney Volunteers,
Ours is a happy little home.
He wakes us up in the middle of the night
And says we must all be prepared to fight.
He puts poor Mother in the dustbin,
To be on sentry guard,
While me and brother John,
With our little nightshirts on,
Are drilling in the old backyard.'

We both made many attempts to alter the ending so that it would be more suitable for a couple of girls to sing, but never managed it to our own satisfaction.

That's why my father wasn't on parade with the rest of the Volunteers but with me at the window when they were lined up on the Square one Sunday to be inspected by the Duke of Marlborough. I was very excited at the thought of seeing a real Duke, but found he was wearing khaki like everybody else, except — yes, there was a difference! Yes, indeed there was.

'Look!' I cried. 'Look! The Duke's wearing one black boot and one brown one!'

At first I might have been the little boy who pointed out that the Emperor wore no clothes, but the grown-ups took another look and had to agree.

The Duke really was wearing one black boot and one brown one, and yet he was the Inspector who had come to see that our Volunteers were properly dressed, clean and tidy. How did he come to be wearing odd boots himself? I'm still wondering, but I don't suppose there is anyone left who could tell us now.

94

We saw more than a Duke. The Square welcomed a real Princess. A house in High Street had been taken over for the YMCA and Princess Helena Victoria came to open it. She was a daughter of Queen Victoria and aunt of the reigning King, George V, in honour of whose coronation that long procession had walked through the town three years before the war started, with me stubbornly plodding in the middle of it.

My idea of a Princess came from fairy tales, tempered by pictures of our own teenage Princess Mary and the Tsar of Russia's four daughters, but it was an elderly and portly lady in black who walked along the red carpet into the Corn Exchange. I forgave her for looking so dull because, even if she had worn a gown with a train and a golden coronet over golden curls, she couldn't have been treated more respectfully by the ladies and gentlemen who had put on their best clothes to greet her. There was one real lady, so real that she was called 'Lady' instead of 'Mrs', who wore a long white dress in embroidered muslin and a huge black hat, and swept a low curtsey to the Princess, down there on the pavement, in the Square, under my very nose.

It was my special little side window which allowed me to see Her Royal Highness so well, and it gave me a good view of Church Green where a hotel housed German prisoners of war. 'EINGANG VERBOTEN' said a notice in bold black print over the front door. I was told it meant you couldn't go in, but I thought it unreasonable to put up a notice in German to keep out people like me when it would have made more sense to tell the German prisoners that they must stay in.

But they didn't stay in. Some of them were hired out to help local farmers, who were responsible for fetching them and taking them safely back. Any day I cared to look in holiday time I could see the trap driven up to the hotel by a boy who, I thought, must be about ten years old. He was the prisoner's escort. Out would come his prisoner, climb in and sit by the child's side, and more often than not take the reins and drive away. Mother and Father were always amused by the small boy, but I envied him because he was doing real war work. There were times when I longed to have brass buttons to polish and a gun to shoot Germans from a trench, but the best I could do was to give our new puppy the patriotic name of Britannia. She became my very own, my constant companion throughout my school days, and we called her Brit for short. I should have liked to do something else as well since Lord Kitchener's eyes caught mine and his finger pointed straight at me over the words 'Your Country Needs You', on a board leaning against a shop front not far from school.

Shopping ought to have counted as war work. Because rationing didn't start until the war was three years old, getting supplies was much more chancy than it became in the Second World War, when it started at once. Success depended on persistence and luck and took so long that, as the one with most time on her hands, I often had to help. I was handicapped by being stupidly shy and having to stand outside every shop door until I had gathered up enough courage to go in. Surely that was worse than fighting Germans!

Mother once asked me to buy a box of matches, urging me to try absolutely everywhere as she needed it so badly. Without a match she couldn't light the gas cooking-stove, or the fire in the grate, or the geyser in the bathroom with its frightening 'pop!' Starting at the grocer's opposite, and going into every likely shop, I worked my way out of the Square, down one side of High Street and back the other, asking everywhere in a timid voice, 'Please, can you let Mother have a box of matches?'

I arrived back in the Square with empty hands. Shopping was horrible, but failure was worse. I decided to try our next door neighbour, the hairdresser, because I knew he sold tobacco and perhaps matches might go with that. Desperately I pushed open the door and went in. Behind the counter, minding shop, was a boy not much bigger than me. I wasn't afraid of him and spoke boldly, 'I want six boxes of Swan Matches.' The boy hesitated, then called through to his father, presumably busy with scissors in the Gents' Saloon.

'Dad,' he said, 'can you let Mithith Ranthom have thix bocthith of Thwan Matchith?'

'Yes, yes, yes, my boy. Of course.'

Heaven had opened! I ran home with six boxes as well as an adventure story.

There were shortages in our shop too. Once a lady came in and asked Father if he had any really good toilet paper; she had been trying all over the town and could only find rubbish. Father said he was sorry that he had only very poor quality too, and he didn't think there would be anything better until the war was over.

'Thank you,' said the lady, turning away rather haughtily. 'Then I'll wait.'

When soldiers were billeted in the town, two of them came to stay with us. We didn't see a great deal of them, but Mother had some extra cooking to do, using the rations they brought in. Mother was a marvellous cook but, 'What *can* I do with this?' I would hear her cry in despair after she had unwrapped a lump of meat which even I could see looked nastier than meat usually did.

One of the soldiers was an Irishman, and my sister and I so much enjoyed listening to him that when our little Jo's next puppy was born he was named Paddy in our friend's honour.

German prisoners were not the only interesting foreigners to be seen in our Square. While they lived in a former hotel, Portuguese labourers were billeted in what had been our Workhouse. Portugal was not fighting, so there were still plenty of men over there, and some of them came to do the work left behind by our own soldiers and sailors. The Workhouse building had to be altered and different equipment provided before they arrived. My grandfather, the ironmonger in the Square opposite the Cinema, was concerned in these renovations, and one day I found in the yard behind his shop a pile of pieces of wood which were all about seven inches square and three quarters of an inch thick. Naturally I asked what they were and was told they were trenchers, a kind of wooden plate, and Grandfather pointed out that not only were they scooped out in the middle to hold the food, they had a small cavity in the rim to hold the salt. They had been thrown out of the Workhouse, and not before it was time, he thought. I agreed, thinking them disgusting, soaked in grease and not fit to be touched. Doubtless they were all destroyed. The other day I saw in a magazine a picture of just such a trencher as these, which was being offered for sale at £225.

The Portuguese when they came were conspicuous, partly because most of their suits were so patched they might almost have been made out of patchwork counterpanes. They were said to draw knives on one another and on anyone else at the slightest provocation. I didn't see this happen but it was also whispered that they smelt, and I could vouch for that. It was a peculiar smell, so shopkeepers used to open both back and front doors quietly to get a good draught through when Portuguese customers had been in.

Very early in the war Belgian refugees had arrived. There were women, children, and old men. They soon became part of our daily lives, but at first we used to stare at them because it wasn't only the women who were in deep black with long flowing veils; quite young girls wore this mourning too and we weren't used to seeing children looking like baby widows. Sometimes they were visited by relatives in the Belgian Army, so there were interesting new uniforms to look at.

There was one old man with the longest white beard I had ever seen who used to come to our house and talk about the war, and his adventures as a refugee, in mixed-up French and English. He was called 'Professor' and used to draw pictures for me, comic ones of Kaiser Bill and the Crown Prince, usually called 'Little Willie' in comic pictures in the newspapers. Another Belgian became a teacher at the Grammar School and took drawing, not French as you might think, and another was the attendant at our Swimming Bath, which was really a piece of the river with cabins and diving-boards built on the bank.

Some of the Belgian children came to my school, where we were told to make friends with them, always to be kind and to speak French as much as we could. The results were sometimes unfortunate, especially for one little boy who had brought some fruit to eat at playtime and became very puzzled indeed. Three children who had spent some time earnestly composing a sentence in French and deciding that just one English word in it couldn't matter very much, advanced on him bravely with his conversational opening: 'Avez-vous mangé votre pear?'

'Hein? Hein?' gasped the startled little Belgian, for it really was no fit question to put to a child who had probably lost his father, and was quietly eating fruit from a paper bag.

The war was nearly ended when, with my little Brit, now fully grown, I watched newly-arrived German prisoners being marched along to 'Eingang Verboten', as we called the Fleece Hotel. One of them was carrying a canary in a cage, which seemed a funny thing to have brought from the trenches. 'Old men and boys. They look finished,' said my father. He sounded sad.

Not long afterwards the war was finished and I rushed home on Armistice Day. One of the sisters had come into my classroom and whispered to the one teaching us. They were both excited, but you could never tell with grown-ups; the secret might have been something quite dull or down right silly. Not until the end of the lesson, when it was time to go home at midday, were we told that the war had ended at eleven o'clock that morning and our side had won. We rushed into the Square to find flags already flying and I burst into our shop.

'Dad,' I said, 'everyone else has put up flags. Why haven't we?'

'My dear,' he replied quietly, 'we've left them for you to put up so that you can tell your grandchildren about it.'

That was something nice to look forward to, but the flags must go up at once. I was soon dashing from window to window, pulling a mass of assorted flags from a box Mother had dragged down from the attic, and with her help thrusting them out into the Square on long bamboo poles. They were the same ones we'd used for the coronation. I hoped my sister, now away at boarding school, had a flag to put up, or what about her grandchildren?

The Square looked very gay on that eleventh of November, 1918, but once the flags were up there was really nothing else to do and it all seemed rather flat. Certainly there was no question of going back to school. Some boys formed themselves into a band and marched through the Square blowing through combs and banging on dustbin lids. That was fine, but soon over. Surely something must be happening, somewhere? I tied red, white and blue ribbons to the collars of Brit and her mother Jo and took them out to look for something — anything. There was nothing, except a lot of people out in the street walking about and talking. Some of them were crying. Grown-ups!

So for me the Square's celebration with flags, combs and dustbins marked the end of the Great World War to end all wars. Twenty-seven years later, when we were celebrating the end of the Second World War, the Square was a very lively place indeed, but that is another story.

ABOVE: Parading in the Market Square; BELOW: marching off down The Hill. (Both WTR)

PART II.

Gladys Davidson's Patriotic success

"BRITANNIA'S REVUE,"

Produced under the direction of

G. DUDLEY BARLOW.

Characters :

Britannia—MURIEL ABRAHAM.	Jack Tar—A. P. HOLTOM.
Scotland—HILDA LEIGH.	Aeroplane—MABEL CATTELL.
Ireland— NANCIE PENSON.	John Bull—R. R. BROAD.
Wales—ENA LIST.	Tommy Atkins—C. R. S. LOXLEY.
Red Cross Nurse—GLADYS BLAKE	English Rose—LILIAN HOLTOM.

Rosebuds — { DOROTHY BARTLETT. JESSIE BARTLETT.
KATHLEEN RANSOM. RITA LEIGH.

Farm Girl—GLADYS BLAKE.

Munition Girl—ETHEL FLOREY.

Father Time—E. S HOLTOM.

COLONIES :

Canada—HAROLD ABRAHAM.	India—KATHLEEN WALKER.
Australasia FRED G. ALDEN.	South Africa—D. S. H PEARMAN.

West Indies—E. W. PICKFORD.

ALLIES :

France—MAMIE BROAD & NANCIE PENSON.

Russia—DAISY WILSDON & DOREEN CLACK.

Belgium—ENA LIST & HILDA LEIGH.

Serbia—SYBIL NISBET.

Japan—GLADYS. BLAKE.

Italy—NITA WEEKS & R. P. ABRAHAM.

Roumania—DOROTHY WEEKS.

History—ETHEL PASMORE.   Hope—MIDGE CLOWSER & NANCIE PENSON.

Peace—MOLLIE SANDERS.

SCENE :— BRITANNIA'S RECEPTION HALL.

100   DANCES arranged by MISS NANCIE PENSON.

Army Form B. 55.

Great Britain and Ireland.

Applicable only during the emergency commencing on 4th August, 1914.

To the OCCUPIER (name) *W. J. Ransom Esq*
(See Note A).

at *14. West Hill* Street, in the Parish of *Witney*

    In accordance with the provisions of the Army Act you are hereby required to find Quarters for—

OFFICERS AND MEN—

    Class I.   .... Lodging and Attendance for _____ officers _____ men

    Class II.   .... Lodging and Attendance for __*2*__ men

    Class III.   .... Unfurnished Accommodation for _____ officers _____ men

    The Military Authorities are empowered to call upon you to provide meals as well as quarters for soldiers.

HORSES—

    Class I.   .... Proper Stabling with forage for _____ horses

    Class II.   .... Proper Stabling without forage for _____ horses

    Class III.   .... Covered Accommodation only for _____ horses

of the *R.F.C.* Regiment, from _____ to _____ (if period known).

    Dated the *4th* day of *March* 19*18*

James Smith Capt Billet Master.   101

Overleaf are shown :—

    The accommodation to be provided under each class.

    The quantities of food and drink to be supplied to soldiers (if you are to supply meals) as fixed by His Majesty's Regul...

    The rates of payment for acco...

NOTE A.—In time of
stables ...

OPPOSITE: Red Cross concert programme, 1917. ABOVE: Billeting notice, 1918. BELOW: My sister made a copy of a popular cartoon, 1915. The Kaiser's and Hitler's moustaches were a gift to cartoonists. (All PR)

THE ARMISTICE IS SIGNED !

A SERVICE OF THANKSGIVING

WILL BE HELD IN

The Wesleyan Church,

TO-NIGHT AT 7-30.

ABOVE: 1918: a German bomber, captured in Salonika, stands among the sheep in the Market Square, raising funds to make aeroplanes for us. The Corn Exchange railings, on the left, were taken down in the next World War, when metal was needed to make more weapons. (MF)
BELOW: Thanksgiving service leaflet, Armistice Day, 11 November, 1918. (PR)

Hitler's War

In the summer of 1934 my sister and I were a long way from the Square. We had gone with a party from the National Union of Students to see the Passion Play at Oberammergau and to spend the rest of the holiday being shown round a number of university cities by German students. We found these wearing either the brown uniform of Hitler's Storm Troopers or the black one of his élite corps, the Black Guards.

Towards the end of the holiday, when I was happily tracing on a wall-map of Europe the route we had been following, one of our Storm Trooper escort joined me and said, so casually that it made my blood run cold, 'The next war will start there.' His finger rested on the Polish Corridor, the strip of land which gave Poland access to the sea at the port of Danzig.

Five years later it happened.

An elderly customer came into the shop, handed in her prescription and sank down heavily onto the chair.

'Eavy fighting,' she said. ''Eavy fighting in Poland. It's all on the posters down the street.''Eavy fighting. In Poland. 'Eavy fighting. Lord, 'ow I do sweat,' and she gave the brim of her hat such a blow with the back of her hand that it took a backwards leap and formed a halo for her face. The hat had a tall crown with flowers climbing towards the summit. I can never think of the outbreak of the Second World War without picturing incongruously both the pointing finger in Nuremburg and this decorative headgear on the other side of our counter.

I looked out into the Square where all that long time ago the Duke of Marlborough had stood in odd boots reviewing the Volunteers, and a dustbin lid band had welcomed the coming of peace. Was it to be filled with khaki uniforms again?

War had almost flared up at the Crisis in 1938, when the Square had seen the distribution of gasmasks, but had been waved away with a flourish of Neville Chamberlain's scrap of paper on his return from a meeting with Hitler. That had been just a year ago, and it was not long before the country was expecting it to flare up again and believing that, instead of a deadly stalemate in trenches, there would be a swift decision in the air. It was thought that instant bombing

103

would cause immense destruction and enormous casualties and we'd been told it would be a good idea to prepare a room as a shelter.

On Sunday, two days after Hitler's attack on Poland, my mother, father, sister, and I sat round the radio while the gloomy voice of Neville Chamberlain announced that 'a state of war' existed between Germany and us. He had scarcely finished speaking before there came the wail of that famous first air raid warning. Clearly, we thought, everything was already going according to plan, so we trooped into the room we called our air raid shelter.

It was an upstairs room and we called it a shelter for no better reason than that we'd had shutters made to fit the windows. These were supposed to stop glass flying about in case of a hit. They were good shutters and when joined together made a good draught screen after the war.

Wondering where the raids were, we sat there solemnly until the All Clear sounded; afterwards we learned that the alarm had been a mistake. There had been no raids anywhere. I believe we spent one more Alert in that 'shelter' before deciding, as other people did, not to bother again unless something really seemed to be happening, and that saved a lot of time. When something did happen in the town and two bombs fell on Church Green, most people were in bed and everything was over in a few seconds. That was when our shop window was blown out.

The rest of that first Sunday we spent fixing up blackout curtains at all the windows. We might not have burdened ourselves in our home with such Heath Robinson arrangements had we guessed how many times we should be putting them up and taking them down, but at least they didn't provoke any complaints from Air Raid Wardens. Everybody was laughing at the story going the rounds about the old lady who had blacked out only the front windows of her cottage. When taken to task by a Warden she had protested, 'But Hitler will never come in at the back, will he?'

Another favourite precaution was sticking strips of gummed paper on window panes. I had some bright yellow strips which I stuck in a diamond-shaped latticework pattern over the shop window, and as this was the style usually chosen it gave the Square a distinctly Olde Worlde appearance, while making the inhabitants confident that they had protected themselves against the flying glass of the modern world.

Two incidents belonging to the first few days of War stand out in my memory. One is the passing through the Square of a long procession of commandeered commercial vans and lorries; many of them, besides bearing the names and addresses of northern firms, had some slogan scrawled on them in chalk. 'FIRST STOP DANZIG' was the favourite, for those were the days when we were going to pass straight through the Siegfried Line without stopping to hang any washing on it. Danzig was years farther away than any of us suspected.

The other is the assembling of our Territorials in the Square, ready to be driven off to camp. 'Be you afeard?' one young volunteer was asked by his mate. 'I dunno if you'd call it being afeard,' was the carefully considered reply, 'but I bin somewhur six times this marning.'

Then business took a curious turn. It seemed that the town had suddenly become vermin-conscious as people rushed in to buy 'something for things in the hair'. Child evacuees from London had been distributed round local families and had brought many problems with them. This one was tackled so enthusiastically that soon we had no suitable vermin-killers left to offer, nor could we obtain further stocks from the London warehouses which used to supply us, so great had been the demand from all the Safety Areas where the children had been dispersed. Of all things, in our shop it was vermin-killer which became the first product to be described in that wartime phrase which everyone grew to loathe and we to avoid — 'in short supply'.

Evacuees became one of the chief topics of conversation over the counter as the Square was gazed upon by eyes used to the streets of London, town children and country people struggled to settle down together, and each was astonished at the other's way of life. As the siren didn't sound again for nearly two months, many people decided to take their children home again, and there was a constant coming and going according to the fortunes of war for as long as it lasted. It was spoken of as Phoney when we were waiting for Hitler to move against the West after his defeat of Poland, then his lightning move through Europe silenced us and we were shocked to hear our army was trapped in France.

One afternoon, when I was arranging something in the shop window, my eye was caught by movement outside the hotel across the Square. A number of officers were getting out of a car and I wondered what they could have been doing to get so filthy and dishevelled. Then a car backfired and in an instant they were all lying flat on the pavement.

'There's something wrong here,' I said, beckoning the others to come and look, but the officers as quickly stood up again and laughed as they went into the hotel.

Suddenly our shop was filled with filthy and dishevelled soldiers, all wanting to buy soap and razors, all wanting to know where they could wash themselves and clean their boots. We found we were meeting men whom the big and little boats had brought home from Dunkirk.

We showed them up to our bathroom and the way down again into the kitchen, where Mother made tea, fed them with whatever we happened to have, and gave them the freedom of our shoebox.

The men sat and ate, or sat and polished their boots, in a dazed sort of way, talking so much that we became half dazed too. One man who had better control of himself than most of them did his best to shut the others up, when he thought their descriptions or their words were too vivid for our ears, but my sister told him not to bother and he was glad to relax. The usual family photos were produced from wallets unusually battered, and there was one man who proudly displayed a worthless framed snapshot of goodness knows whom which he had picked up on a French road, goodness knows why. Every now and then someone would stand up and drift back through the shop into the Square, or another man wander down from the bathroom like a sleepwalker. Scenes like this were going on in homes all over the town.

A clergyman who found two soldiers at a street corner arguing over a piece of paper asked if he could help them.

'Yes, mate. Where are we now?'

He told them. The name of the town didn't register, nor did the name of the county. Guessing the root of the trouble he said,

'You are in England, you know.'

'The hell we are,' one man retorted angrily.

'Here, stow it,' said the other. 'Can't you see the chap's a bloody parson?' and he handed over the piece of paper, which turned out to have written on it the name and address of the family which was going to put them up for the night.

The next morning we could see the men assembled on Church Green in blazing sunshine. Tables had been set up covered with clothes and equipment and they were being kitted out afresh.

I remember lugging a heavy portable radio into the shop and the suspense with which we waited with our customers to hear if we were going to fight on after the collapse of France or not. Fired by Churchill's words, we were in the mood to bombard with bottles any Nazi who ventured into the Square, and when the Battle of Britain was being fought we were glad to be invited to take part in it. We fought with our saucepans. We fought with anything else we happened to have which was made of aluminium. Lord Beaverbrook had said this was wanted for Spitfires and, as I crossed the Square, one among many laden people, with all the aluminium things I could lay my hands on, I felt sure we were making a tangible contribution to another fighter aircraft. We weren't always logical about it. One of the Square's housewives, according to her husband, handed in every aluminium saucepan she possessed and then went to a nearby shop to buy a new set. She felt entitled to keep this, Spitfire or no Spitfire.

That was the plane our imagination seized upon. We liked the idea of putting more in the sky and, in common with the rest of the country, our town engaged in scheme after scheme for raising money. A favourite method was the old one of a raffle; raffling something 'in short supply' was often linked with giving a boost to National Savings.

It was easy to do this in a shop, and one of the articles we raffled in this way was a tin of talcum powder, then selling for about three and sixpence but so very difficult to come by that it made an attractive prize. For the price of sixpence we gave a ticket and a sixpenny savings stamp, so the customer lost nothing. We had to explain this very carefully to one lady, and were surprised when she produced her sixpence because we believed her to be opposed to any form of gambling and were sure she would regard this one as sinful.

She did. Accepting the savings stamp but waving the ticket aside, she said, 'I don't approve of raffles so I'll just take this,' picked up the tin of talcum powder and turned towards the door. An irreplaceable prize simply couldn't be allowed to disappear like that. By the time the tin was back on the counter it would have been hard to say which of us was the more embarrassed.

Market Day was frequently chosen for auctioning goods in the Square for 'Spitfire Weeks' or other special efforts. Quite valuable things such as good and scarce pieces of furniture went to the highest bidder, who frequently could afford to offer a high price since he was given the value of his bid in Savings Bonds as well. Often the goods were given back and auctioned again; they could theoretically change hands many times quite quickly and the crowd enjoyed the fun. Of course there was nothing to stop the eventual buyer keeping his purchase and cashing the Bonds, but by the time everyone woke up to this the novelty had worn off. Probably the chief value had been letting us feel we were doing something to stop 'that there Hitler'.

Processions did us good too and brought a little cheerfulness during these special weeks. All wearing the uniform proper to our war work, we marched along that traditional mile from one end of the town to the other. Usually one military or airforce band led the procession and another brought up the rear, and heaven help you if you were somewhere in the middle and tried to march to both. The saluting base was usually in the Square, where the dignitary and his supporters stood on a small platform in the middle by the lamp-post.

The only time an attack of 'flu did me any good was when it kept me out of a procession, so that I watched it from the window and saw something I should have been sorry to miss. One of the town's best known characters, one we were proud of because his very name raised expectation of laughter, a big strong fellow whose mind was not quite as other men's minds are, nearly caused havoc among the Red Cross contingent when he pushed into the marching lines just ahead of its lady Superintendent. He was wearing a tin hat with his initials in large white letters on the front. Goodness only knows how he came by it.

107

At the Superintendent's command 'Eyes left!' a long bony finger jerked up and poked respectfully at the tin hat. I'm certain that the question the Admiral on the platform shot at the worthy by his side concerned what branch of the war effort the lone, gangling figure represented under the initials G.W.

This same figure appeared one day in our shop, stood looking at us for a few moments, and then jerked out in a gruff voice a request which even coming from him was surprising.

'Will you tie me up for the Council?'

We made further enquiries and found that he wished to have his wrist bandaged and the Council would pay for it. This last point was very strongly emphasised as he claimed to have been injured by the dustcart.

My sister, who had a row of Red Cross certificates to support her, quite enjoyed exercising her skill with a crêpe bandage, to which he was quite welcome, but at the end of the month I couldn't resist sending in a formal account to the UDC:

'To tying up G . . . W . . ., Esq.,   1/6'

In came the Surveyor, waving the bill and trying to conceal his mirth as he asked what had been going on, and we learnt that the exceptional strength of someone usually thought unemployable couldn't be wasted in wartime, so our customer had been going round with the dustcart crew to handle heavy bins. He had given several versions of how his wrist came to be injured, and the Surveyor added to his collection the one given to us though he clearly had mental reservations about them all.

After Dunkirk the possibility of an invasion was very much in our minds and no one was much surprised when the warning was given. Church bells all over the country had been silenced when the war started and were to be heard again only as an invasion signal until it ended, so one summer night when our bells jangled the services were alerted and people jumped out of bed to rush to their defence posts.

One of the Home Guard, running to go on duty, was hailed by an old man leaning out of a bedroom window.

'How far have they got?' he was asked.

Happily they had got nowhere; it was a mistake, just as the first Air Raid Warning had been, but there was no rest for the Home Guard.

One Sunday morning I came off night duty at the Report Centre longing for fresh air, so I went home, abandoned my tin hat, collected my terrier puppy and took him into a nearby field. There I sat down and not surprisingly fell asleep. I was woken up by an appalling noise near my ear. Pip had all four feet planted firmly on my chest and was barking with as much ferocity as he could muster. With difficulty I sat up and found he was challenging the Home

Guard, who were creeping along the hedge, and their officer, who continued to advance upon me in the face of this opposition.

'Wouldn't you like to move?' he called. 'We're just going to put up a smoke screen and the wind will bring it towards you.'

I soothed my tiny protector and we went home to breakfast, unsmoked. It would be fun to see the balloon into which 'Dad's Army' could swell this incident.

In the shop we continued to struggle with ration books, and goods which were almost unobtainable or on special permits. To cheer us up I'd pinned a *Punch* cartoon behind the dispensing counter. It showed the not unusual combination of timid little man and haughty clerk in an office. The little man was asking, 'Please, may I have a permit to apply for a permit?'

'At least we haven't come to that,' we comforted ourselves, but before long we had come to that. We had to obtain a doctor's certificate before we could apply for a permit to order a hot water bottle for a customer. It took a long time and what happened to the patient in the meanwhile we didn't care to dwell on.

The representative of one firm explained that we couldn't have the quantity of some unrationed goods that we needed 'because allocations are made on a pre-war basis'. In other words, babies' rusks were still being sent to areas from which babies had been taken away when it would have been more sense to send them to the Safety Areas where the infants actually were.

With this explanation I tried to placate the next customer who found we had no babies' rusks left. Quite rightly she wasn't placated at all but highly indignant and she produced a shattering idea. 'I think all the people who have come here because of the war and don't really belong should be made to do their shopping by post from the shops they used to go to.' The more I considered this idea the more my brain reeled.

I remember one particular customer who would have been affected by this regulation. She had shopped with us regularly since coming into the district and, as we had had no occasion to ask her name, we called her Mrs Canary Slacks among ourselves. One day, when she was buying something needing coupons, the conversation took a turn which led me to fire a broadside against Board of Trade regulations, saying they were difficult enough to remember, let alone carry out. She was strangely silent.

The following week a customer we had known for years asked us to give her 'Mrs Wilson's usual'.

'Which Mrs Wilson would that be?' I asked, hoping for a clue as my mind raced round various Wilson families and their purchases.

'Oh, you know,' was the reply. 'The one that her husband is the Board of Trade.'

'Does she wear yellow trousers?' I was inspired to ask.

'That's right.'

No wonder Mrs Canary Slacks hadn't chimed in with my attack on that Board as almost any other customer would have done, since she was married to its President and was Mrs Harold, the wife of a future Prime Minister.

For the sake of convenience we had nicknames for quite a number of people whose names we didn't know — apart from those given for other reasons! — and these were generally based on something the customer usually wore, or bought, or said. The ones that spring first to my mind are Mrs Wide Sleeves, Miss Germolene and Mrs My-daughter-says. To finish name dropping I will mention one more real one.

One morning when I was out in the Square and up a ladder, washing the shop window — I think all the bright yellow paper latticework had come off by this time — a soldier we knew asked me why I was looking so amused.

'Am I? Well, wouldn't you be if you had just directed a friend of Hitler's to the Ladies'?'

'Not Unity Mitford?'

'No other.'

'Where's my rifle?' he asked, dramatically posing with an imaginary one and carrying on in the 'bang-bang' way beloved of all small boys.

The War was growing into an old war when the Square took on both a new look and a new sound as men in American uniform discovered it. There they were, sitting on the kerb throwing dice, watched by small boys interested in chewing-gum; sauntering along, very conscious of being followed by not so small girls fascinated by hearing in their own streets the accents associated with the dream world of Hollywood, and striding into the shops with their new shopping vocabulary, invariably beginning, 'Say, do you carry so-and-so?' Their manner was quite different too, for when they asked for luxuries they were not expecting to receive 'No' for an answer, and that was something we hadn't met for a long time. It could be refreshing or maddening, according to the mood one was in.

As they came from a land of plenty, shortage in shops was something which these young men could not understand, and there we stood behind the counter, long inured to the 'I'm sorry to trouble you as I'm sure it's a silly question but I was just wondering if by any chance you happened to have so-and-so?' kind of approach. On our side we were trying to think up new ways of saying that we were sorry we had none left, and we were all used to our very advertisements having gone into battledress. No longer able to urge us to buy their goods, advertisers set out to keep them in our minds and hope in our hearts, so that a Stork sitting on a packet of margarine would proclaim, 'Victory brings nearer the day when I'll return', an aproned cobbler assured us that 'Phillips Rubber Soles and Heels are Worth Waiting For', and a cooker radiated Churchillian confidence with its ringing cry, 'The Day will Dawn when Esse Cookers are available for all homes'. A printed advertisement advising us 'Never pass a shop which sells Bourjois — its quota of "Evening in Paris" may just have arrived!' was useless to a young American expecting to walk out of the shop there and then with a handsome bottle of perfume elegantly giftwrapped, just as if Hitler had never been heard of.

Sometimes their confidence could have been expressed more tactfully. An immensely tall young man — and it seemed to us that GI's ran to excessive height or excessive girth — towered over us, so that we had to crick our necks to look at him as he introduced himself with, 'Waal, we had to come over and win the last war for you and now I guess we've had to come over to win this one for you too.' As a conversational opening, this well-meant effort was not an outstanding success, and he little knew how near he came to having bottles whirling round his head.

Shops which didn't 'carry' so many of the goods asked for, and didn't wrap up the ones they could supply, seemed to make these visitors nervous of buying English products. One soldier who rang our Urgent Medicine bell round about midnight required aspirins, and had a long story, long since forgotten, to explain why it was essential for him to have them at once. When, speaking from the window above the bell, I said that we did carry them and I would come down and get some for him, he cautiously asked if I had a certain American brand. I named the well-known English makes we stocked but suddenly the matter had become less urgent and he guessed he wouldn't trouble me to get them after all.

The police had advised us not to answer the bell during the night, but we had been accustomed to answering it at whatever hour it rang the whole night through and thought it would not be right to stop. We did first sum up the caller and the situation from the upstairs window, and there was one night when I didn't go down. A very drunk and vociferous GI was demanding 'medicinal alcohol', urgently needed, he declared. 'Come on. Come on down. Come on, come on. Alcohol — I need it. Sure, I need it. Come on. Come on down. I need alcohol.' I felt his more urgent need was for the rainwater butt which our trespassing paratrooper had inadvertently found to be so beneficial, but I didn't feel capable of introducing him to it.

In the course of time an air raid shelter appeared on the bank in the Square and gave us some confidence, though I never heard of anyone actually using it. One air raid casualty came into the shop for treatment and we advised her to go to the Surgery. This lady had spent the previous night in a London air raid shelter and was busily knitting when a violent bomb blast drove one of the needles clean

111

through her finger. It seemed a curious achievement for the crew of the plane which had come over to drop that particular bomb.

The war brought us opportunities to see pictures and hear music which would never have come to the Corn Exchange in peace time. To our shame the Celebrity Concerts were poorly attended and the hall was filled only when Myra Hess brought her warm personality with her art, and lifted our hearts with a fine programme ending in *Jesu joy of man's desiring*, which will be associated with her for as long as she is remembered.

Owen Brannigan told us it was not the first time he had sung in our hall. Before the war he had been working near the town, competed in one of our Musical Festivals and been told by the adjudicator that he ought to take up singing professionally, so here he was again.

Kathleen Ferrier not only gave her lovely voice to the audience but delighted her hostess.for that night by singing happily about the house. She bubbled over with stories about the beginning of her career, explaining how she had been unable to afford expensive dresses, so her sister had made some from Liberty's upholstery materials, which had looked wonderful on the stage. The face above the breakfast tray taken to her bed was greeted with a heartfelt 'Thank you, love,' and the house echoed to her songs as she dressed. It was a pity the hens in the garden couldn't see her pleasure when she was given some of their eggs to take home.

CEMA sent us several art exhibitions, so that we could see not only familiar forms such as portraits and landscapes but samples of the new art, then startling. When it was quiet in the shop I would sometimes slip next door for a few minutes at a time, and gaze in some astonishment at collages composed of paint, pieces of newspaper, scraps of metal, dress material and bits of string all within one frame, or at abstracts conforming to the general rule that their swirls of colour must not look like anything. Many of us were quite lost but glad to have something new to look at and argue about besides the twin topics of war and food — the very reason why these exhibitions were on the road.

During one of my visits I was severely reprimanded by the young woman who had come with the pictures because she'd heard me say there were few on the walls I could bear to live with. 'That is no way to judge a picture,' she said sternly. I could only reply that the title of the exhibition, 'Pictures to Live With', invited this judgement. She begged me to go to her lecture that evening, when she was going to explain everything.

I went, and so did a handful of other people. We sat informally round the lecturer in a corner of the Corn Exchange hall and heard her say that the medium of art must be appropriate to its subject, and that was why she could not bear to see hard alabaster carved into the semblance of soft lace on effigies. It was an unfortunate illustration; she was immediately taken up by an elderly gentleman convinced that if she could only see the lace on some particular effigies he admired, she would immediately change her mind. As he was both kind and helpful, with a lofty disregard for the difficulties of going anywhere at all in wartime, he set about directing her to the church where these tombs could be found. In vain did she try to bring to an end the account of how you turned to the right at this pub, and to the left after that bridge, such directions being necessary because all signposts had been taken down to confuse any nuns in boots and other enemy parachutists.

Most members of the audience were familiar with their fellow townsman's enthusiasms and helpfulness, knew it was no use struggling against the tide of information, and that when he'd run down he would probably take a nap. The lecturer gamely went on trying to lecture, but the route to the alabaster effigies was still unwinding itself when the siren went and I had to snatch up my tin hat and run to the Report Centre as fast as the blackout would let me. There was nothing much for me to do when I got there, which was a good thing, but the Alert meant that I remained in ignorance of modern art and had to content myself with becoming accustomed to it.

We had all become accustomed to a great many things and the war seemed to have been going on for ever when we found that there really were blue birds over the white cliffs of Dover, and flags flying in the Square again.

Down came our venerable box from the attic and up went the Union Jacks and Naval Ensigns at the windows where they had been flown on every occasion of rejoicing for the past forty years. We stood out in the Square admiring them, and then caught sight of the Union Jack which the Council was flying from the Corn Exchange balcony. It looked as if it had gone into the Ark to support the pair of moths invited to fly up that gangway.

It chanced that the next customer who came in was the Surveyor, so my sister offered him a packet of moth balls, suggesting the Council might like to amuse itself trying to throw them through the holes. He took one look at the flag, gasped, and was gone. In a matter of minutes the offending Union Jack had gone too and a brave new one was flying in its place.

There were two days of celebration to end the Second World War — one when the Germans surrendered in May and another in August when the Japanese gave in. After a gap of nearly fifty years the three months' gap has narrowed, and in my mind the two days have merged into one.

The same instinct which took me out with the dogs in a futile search for jollity in 1918 moved the whole town in 1945. People surged out of their houses when evening fell and with one accord made for the Square.

Once there, what should a happy mass of people do but dance? There was little room and at first no music, but everyone seized a partner; men danced with women or men, women danced with men or women, and they danced anything they chose in any way they could. In the denser part of the throng they were simply standing and swaying on their feet. There was one young man who contrived to toss his partner up in the air again and again — no mean accomplishment when the Square was nearly solid with people, who had tossed their cares away and were exulting under the incredible glow of electricity which had not lighted up the streets for the past six years.

Suddenly a hokey-cokey line wriggled out of the shapeless whirl; growing all the time, it snaked away round the two blocks of buildings until it grew tired of that and dissolved into couples again, who went on dancing as if they had forgotten how to stop.

There were others who needed to slake their thirst and who increased the general noise and merriment; window sills were in such demand for resting with a drink that it seemed the plate glass must give way. Someone produced a small cask of home-made wine with bottles and tumblers for serving it in over-generous portions; soldiers seized the cask and paraded with it, singing as they went. The hotel began to worry about its rapidly disappearing glasses — but retrieved a number of them from window sills and odd corners in the morning. As the jollification increased and grew noisier, dancers began to think it was time to go home; lights were switched off behind the happily uncurtained windows, and soon only a few songsters and stragglers were left beneath the idly flapping flags.

To me the most joyful sound to fill the Square was the ringing of the long-silent church bells, since they would go on pealing years after the dancers ceased to spin and the flags had been folded away, but I think the old Square would claim that in the spontaneous rejoicing of that exultant night it had spent its finest hour.

Alpha and omega — ABOVE: Morris Dancers appear in the Square from time to time, usually from nearby Bampton where there is a Society for the Preservation of Ancient Junketing. These were dancing in 1938 — as peace drew to a close. (MF) BELOW: V-E Day 1945: the war in Europe has ended and the dance in the Market Square has just begun. It warmed up! (TW)

115

Peace Breaks Out

Over forty years have gone by since the Square was filled with this massed dancing, though the flags have flown again for the Coronation and Silver Jubilee of Queen Elizabeth II and I have seen that lady herself being driven slowly through the Square. For over half that time I have not been living in it, but a crow would not take long to fly, or even walk, from the site of my old front door to where the present one swings open. Life there became diminished during the years following the war because so many other people drifted away too. The sheep have gone altogether.

In my time the Square was chiefly surrounded by buildings where business was carried on downstairs all day while a family lived in the rooms above. At night the upstairs rooms were still alive, their windows bright; downstairs the doorbells pealed and front doors were thrown open to spill light and voices on to the pavement. So much living accommodation has now been turned into offices, or swallowed up by showrooms and storerooms, that after closing time there is a stillness behind the walls when keys have been turned by people who live the rest of their lives elsewhere. Children used to play in gardens at the back, but most of these have been built over, used for parking cars, or simply grown into wildernesses. It is surprising that the general appearance of the Square by day has changed so little; even supermarkets have not made an overwhelming difference.

When the first supermarket opened in the Square during the sixties, I had so many frights in it that I stopped speaking scornfully of shoppers who told magistrates that they really had meant to pay for the goods.

On my first visit, after being bewildered by the choice and then stupefied by the long wait at the paydesk, I stood watching the checkout girl as her fingers flickered and her palm banged on the adding machine. My thoughts had plenty of time to wander off to the laborious way I used to add on fingers hidden in my overall pockets, to the sums hastily worked out on the backs of snatched-up showcards, and from there travelled far away to the alarmingly competent Russian women who took over the bank of my cruising ship when we docked at Leningrad, and changed our pounds into

ABOVE: The British Legion's Annual Carnival was revived for a few years after the Second World War; the Carnival Queen in 1950 was Miss Molly Drake from the Post Office. She is now Mrs Ashley and lives in the USA. (JB) BELOW: The War in the Far East had ended with the surrender of Japan. On V-J Day, 1945 the cinema is celebrating with flags and the central figure is the owner, Mr Huddleston. The cinema was rebuilt in the early thirties and its name, first 'The Electric Theatre' and then 'The People's Palace' is now simply 'The Palace'. (PB)

roubles after smartly snapping beads to and fro on those frames with wires we associate with nurseries.

Suddenly it was my turn. After the machine had received its final bang I was given a brown ticket and some pink stamps, fumbled for my handbag and found I'd tucked it absent-mindedly under my arm. It was accompanied by a packet of tea.

'Oh, there's this as well,' I said feebly, flourishing the packet and wondering how it had got there. More flicks, bangs and stamps — and then a very queer look. What was the girl thinking? I must be more careful.

I was very careful for a time but worse was to come. I had a special purchase to make as a neighbour wanted a packet of pineapple jelly and nothing else would do. Of course there were dozens of jellies in any other flavour but that one. I pushed and pulled with decreasing hope until I was at last rewarded by finding a solitary pineapple lurking at the bottom of a pile at the back, and then went in triumph to the paydesk.

When the girl had slid the goods along the counter in her usual gesture of dismissal I picked the things up — tickets, stamps and money in the purse, purse in the handbag, small things in my pockets, big things in the shopping bag — there was really quite a lot to do, but what was this orange jelly doing in my hand when I'd already packed up the pineapple? Where had it come from?

'I seem to have picked up two jellies instead of one,' I said, and it did sound silly.

'I'll see if I've charged it,' said the girl.

She hadn't, and took the orange one from me. There were some queer looks from the queue and this time I was really worried, for I had absolutely no idea where the packet had been when I passed through Checkpoint Charlie. Could it have been in my pocket? It was an alarming thought.

Still worse was to come. My wire basket was full to the brim and there was nothing left on my shopping list but junket. How could that needle be found in this particular haystack? I asked the girl who was piling soapflakes on a shelf and she said good-naturedly, 'Just by the entrance. You could have seen it as you came in.'

Back to the entrance I went, put the junket on top of the basket with the sense of a job well done, decided I'd just enough time to go to the Post Office, sailed through the doorway, and collided with a woman coming in.

'Why can't people use the proper entrance?' I thought rather crossly, but drew back to let her pass because I'm that sort of person. She didn't pass but stood staring at me with a look of horror on her face. Was there a splodge on mine? Or was something slipping? I looked down to see if anything was about to coil round my ankles and what I saw was a well-filled wire basket. At the same time I realised I had been dashing out through the way in.

118

'Just look what I'm doing!' I said unnecessarily, for no one could have been looking harder. 'Thank goodness I bumped into you or I should have gone right outside!'

'It was a good thing I saw you before the security people did,' was her comment. I wasn't sure I liked the tone of her voice.

By the time I'd worked my way back to the paydesk, my face was flaming till it hurt. Had security people been following me? Would they have believed me? Would the magistrate have believed I didn't mean to lift the things, basket and all?

There was one in my family, so I asked him.

'Of course I shouldn't!' he said. 'That's what they all say.'

I'm still trying to be careful, but one day my good fairy will be sleeping and the magistrate contemplating me. It's a far cry from the days when Mother was offered a chair in the grocery and goods were brought for her inspection.

So some bigger shops, more offices and fewer homes are some of the changes which have overtaken the Square. Another more obvious one is that there are no more hurdles enclosing sheep and pigs: that market, after dwindling and dwindling, was banished to the Corn Exchange Yard and then disappeared altogether. Waiting in the wings was another kind of market, ready to take over. For a long time, every Thursday, there had been stalls along the pavement leading to the Town Hall and round the Buttercross. As soon as the sheep left the centre of the stage, these stalls moved in and held a market twice a week.

That is why cars couldn't park in the Square on Saturdays and Thursdays, why it smelt of fish instead of sheep and pigs, and why it was so much quieter than in the heyday of the auctioneer, whose powerful voice needed none of our new-fangled microphones. It no longer seems such a large wide-open place on those two days for, if you walk down the middle of the Square, it is like walking down a street with shops on either side. If magic brought back my upstairs window and I could stand behind it, I should see little but the back of one row, the roofs of both, and not much of the goods they were selling.

Last time I walked through the market the fish provided the richest smell and the fruit and vegetables the brightest colours, even though on nearby stalls there were both real plants growing in pots and plastic ones in exuberant bloom. I admired the optimism of the man selling belts and bags, who clearly expected to find supporters of Manchester United wherever he set up his stall, and the aplomb of a trader who was stirring a huge mug of tea with a foot-long piece of wood, which had a ticket for 27p/lb slotted into the other end. Someone who originated from a warmer climate had spread a display of dresses over plastic sheets on the ground, while at the other end of the row gowns were hanging on stands arranged to form a coy little cubicle round a mirror. There was a time when

119

these stalls were near the Ladies' Loo underneath the Town Hall and, if they wished, ladies could pop in there to judge the effect of a dress. Those Ladies' and Gents' have left the Square now the Town Hall has been splendidly renovated and turned into Town Council Offices, and the new ones are to be found alongside the new road leading from the ancient Buttercross to the new Shopping Centre. Their new residence has been built in the shape of the Buttercross, the spaces between the pillars discreetly filled with walls, and everything was thought to be vandalproof until the doors were torn off by destructionists determined not to be foiled by any council, designer or architect.

It was logical that from a stall selling live budgies I could also have bought a wide variety of nourishment for pets, ranging from parrot food to puppy meal and coloured dogs' biscuits, but I did wonder how it came about that someone nearby, specialising in toilet goods, was also offering small rugs.

'Sheepskin and calfskin, love,' said the trader who saw me looking quizzically at them. 'Sheepskin and calfskin' — it sounded like a dirge for the vanished Livestock Market. I stood for some time by the next display, fascinated by the advertisements superimposed on looking-glass which used to flourish in pubs. Beefeaters, guardsmen and nouveau art ladies were the people most frequently depicted as enjoying the product offered for sale and, after I'd recovered from my astonishment at finding Coca-Cola recommended as the Ideal Brain Tonic, I suddenly found Lord Kitchener's finger pointing at me again after a gap of some sixty years. Apparently my country still needs me, and I took that shattering thought away.

So there is still life in the old Square, but not for much longer. The Powers have decided that it shall be put to sleep. It has just been declared a Pedestrian Precinct and is threatened with paving stones, low walls, bollards and rails, seats and lighting, to say nothing of a Witney Lamb motif in the centre. This sounds better than an aviary of dispirited birds or the kind of sculpture with holes in it which I have seen in so many Pedestrian Precincts, but I cannot believe the Square is ready for retirement, when all around it people are popping in and out of shops and offices, carrying their money in and out of banks, having their eyes tested and their teeth filled, poring over objects in exhibitions and jumble sales in the Corn Exchange, besides eating and drinking in a pub, hotel, and restaurant which allows you to take away your kebabs and fish and chips if that's the way you like it.

There have been for years seats and trees along the road which skirts the Square. Three seats were conveniently placed for people waiting for the Oxford 'buses until the 'bus-stop was moved a few tantalising yards away, so passengers now sit on the low wall outside Barclay's Bank. Trees line the way down the Hill and there is still one at the corner of the building where the Other Chemist used to

120

be. This little plane has not yet had time to inspire the affection felt for the big elm it replaces. That old tree was loved, but the Dutch Elm Disease got it in the end. Pinned all round the trunk, in true country fashion, were always notices, most of them homemade, advertising such events as special meetings of the Women's Institute, the Boy Scouts and Bangers; Jumble Sales and Football; Discos, Folk Songs and Elizabethan Keyboard Music.

In my childhood an owl hooted at night from among its branches, a sound so familiar that I found it comforting and not in the least alarming. To the end little birds nested there. Not long before it was felled I joined a group of people to find out why they were gazing upwards so intently. A nestling was resting in its own front doorway, which was a hole in the trunk having the impressive shape of a Norman arch. The little creature seemed quite unperturbed by the noise and bustle round the market stalls.

Why should we break so deliberately the old tradition believed to have been established centuries ago, by the countrywomen who sat on the steps of the Buttercross selling butter and other produce brought in from their holdings? A Market Square is not meant to be a place of peace and repose. Next door to ours is Church Green, said to be the length of a bowshot, where archery was practised when that was compulsory for the safety of the realm, and there for years people have been able to sit and contemplate an expanse of grass, trees, flowers, mellow houses and the lovely church. Flowers contemplated in the Market Square should be in pots, for sale between the shoulder bags supporting Manchester United and the Beefeaters advocating London Distilled Gin. Hustle and bustle belong to a Market Square; it is no place for marking time. It should remain the place to which people naturally turn, because they know everyone else will be there when something wonderful happens, like Peace breaking out.

ABOVE: The Square after the war, about 1948. Cars were parked there, except on Market Days. This shows well how the middle part is bounded by the two detached blocks, and the road running past joins High Street outside the Old Post Office, now Denton's. (PR) BELOW: In 1950 the Dagenham Girl Pipers, whose display in the Square was one of the most colourful ever seen there, led the Carnival Procession through the town, after assembling on Church Green. (JB)

ABOVE: In 1968 the shop was demolished to make the entrance to a carpark. For the past ten years the business had belonged to Mr Parry, who bought it from my sister Kathleen. She had been Father's partner for some years when he died in 1942, and continued to run the shop when it became her own. (TW) BELOW: In 1987 the entrance was no longer needed as the carpark could be reached from Witan Way, the new road running parallel to the Market Square and High Street to serve the new Shopping Centre, so builders came to fill the gap. (PB)

Epilogue

It was by an odd chance that my book and what I think of as my Market Square came to an end together. Two big changes in the Square were inevitable; once it had been accepted that Woolgate, the new shopping centre, had to be built behind it, there had to be a footway and a roadway to take shoppers there.

We can now walk under an imposing archway where Cook and Boggis's stood before their disastrous fire in 1964, or drive along a road which destroyed a former coaching inn called the Crown Hotel, which was successively known in my lifetime as Habgood's house, Frost's office and No 27. A long battle was fought to preserve this building, but the car always wins. We have exchanged a handsome old house for a busy and tricky crossroads between the Town Hall and the Buttercross, which makes us wish we had heads swivelling round like an owl's to guide us more safely every time we walk across it.

The twenty-year-old gap next to the Corn Exchange, where our house and shop had stood, has been filled in; cars can now reach the new carparks from the back. The new premises resemble the old ones in general outline and are not yet finished. If you care to peep through a crack in the hoardings there is nothing to be seen yet but an enclosed empty space going much further back than our home did. It includes the ground once covered by the warehouses, the wash-house, the wood shed and probably the two-seater earth closet and pigsty as well. I do hope someone has preserved the great stone slab full of fossils which gave our predecessor's pigs a front wall, and I wonder what has happened to the copper in which our boiling clothes were stirred round with a wooden copper-stick every Monday.

When I wrote the last word of the last chapter and a ruminative pencil lingered on the fullstop dabbed after it, I had been quarrelling with a suggested development for the Market Square. This was not inevitable like the footway and roadway, but a matter of choice. Pedestrianisation was in the air, and if that is wanted it can surely be obtained by putting up a notice telling cars to go away, but

ABOVE: Cook and Boggis's drapery c1905, destroyed by fire in 1964. Waitrose built a supermarket on the site but in 1987 built another in the new shopping centre behind it. (JF) BELOW: The entrance to Woolgate, the new shopping centre, was cut through the group of buildings Waitrose left behind. Jackson's forge used to be where the opticians now are. (PB)

the lengthy word grew into a phrase, 'landscaped into a pedestrian precinct', and many of us began to tremble as the forecasts spoke of trees and seats and walls and bits and pieces all over the Square which might make it look like a piece of municipal parkland.

Now the landscaping has been completed, mercifully the Square is still an open space, but the question 'Why can't they leave it alone?' has changed only to 'Why couldn't they leave it alone?' for the Square seems to have lost the character it had without finding another one.

My first feeling was one of relief when I realised the open space was still there, and my second a throb of joy on greeting the little old-fashioned lamp-post which has replaced the graceless tall one in the centre. After that I had no feelings at all. Blankness set in and I wasn't sure why.

The trees and seats have come. There are five new trees, and it may well be that the great-grandchildren of today's teenagers will be fighting to preserve them against an authority aching to get them gone. There are three new seats facing the road, where never before were seats to rest passengers waiting for 'buses returning from Oxford, and who can object to those? There are posts and railings marking a passage across the Square, some Cotswold stone walling at the Buttercross end to tell cars they are no longer welcome, some litter bins we hope will be used and another little old lamp-post to light our feet down the side road to Woolgate. Everything is set along the sides of the Square so that the market stalls can still trade in the middle twice a week, confounding those among us who had screamed that the promised landscaping would kill the remaining life in the Square stone dead, so what is wrong?

Have I reached the age which opposes all change? I suspect the paving stones. The biggest change is that these cover the whole Market Square like a piazza or patio, and Witney isn't in either Italy or Spain. When I was watching the traders taking down their stalls and one of them threw the metal rods heavily on the ground, I wanted to call, 'Look out! You'll crack the paving stones!' which wouldn't have occurred to me if the stones had seemed to be at home. Another onlooker shook her head. 'It doesn't look right', she said, with a gesture embracing the Square.

The trees may make all seem well when they have grown up and asserted their authority. Meanwhile I am indulging in a pleasant little fantasy and imagining, now there are no cars and not even a horse and cart to worry about, that children will come out to play again. What a surface there would be for spinning tops, bowling hoops, rolling marbles or chalking out hopscotch squares! I wonder if I should be thought old enough to join in, this time round.

ABOVE: In the background is the house which was demolished so that the road could go through to the Woolgate Shopping Centre. The gap to the right is also something gone for ever — the entrance to Langel Lane, or Crown Lane, which led between stone walls festooned with ivy to a footbridge with a turnstile to keep in cattle, and then to a meadow called Langel Common between two arms of the River Windrush. (WTR) BELOW: The new road down to Woolgate, with new loos built in the shape of the Buttercross (background). (PB)

ABOVE: New Square roots: landscaping proceeds; the paving stones have been laid, the posts have arrived (left) and so has the old-fashioned lamp-post (centre). Left of the Corn Exchange, and still partly behind hoardings, are the premises filling the gap where our chemist's shop once stood. BELOW: The seats are in place and square beds have been prepared for the trees. The new building follows the general outline of our old one, but I miss the three dormer windows in the roof and the little side one upstairs looking up Church Green. (Both PB)

ABOVE: The central Square seen from the top of The Hill. The additions are along the sides, leaving the middle clear for the return of the market stalls. BELOW: Room with a view? This is what I would see twice a week if I still had an upstairs window in the Market Square. New trees have not yet been planted. (Both PB)

Index

Subscribers

1 Witney Town Council
2 West Oxfordshire District Council
3 Oxfordshire County Council
4 Oxfordshire County Libraries, Witney Branch

5 Phyllis Ransom
6 Clive & Carolyn Birch
7 Peter Barker
8 Mrs H. Dearnley
9
10 J.B. Crawford
11 Peter Johnson
12 Robert Surman
13 Mrs Valerie Moon
14 Mrs Joy Hollier
15 Denis Morgan
16 Beryl Walter
17 Charles Knight
18 John & Margaret Hirons
19 Mrs Iris State
20 Cyril F.J. Miles
21 Charles & Joan Gott
22 Jennifer Williamson
23 René Knight
24 Mrs Pamela Durham
25 Mrs M.J. Lawley
26 Jean Barton
27 Josephine K. Scott
28 Mrs Mary Winter
29 Miss Jean Izzard
30 Mrs V.R. Chandler
31 Mrs V.H. Leigh
32 A.J. Goodey
33 Mrs P.M. Burbidge
34 Frank Bishop
35 Walter Harris
36 Miss A.M.J. Slack
37 Mrs B.J. Forkner
38 Miss E. Delnevo
39 Victoria & Albert
    Museum
40 London Guildhall
    Library
41
42 Cllr G.M. Fowler
43 Enid M. Griffin
44 D.M. Stoneham
45 Miss J.E. Fletcher
46 F.W. Grant
47 Ken Woodford
48 Mrs P. Roberts
49 Mrs B. Hudson
50 Joan Phillips
51 Mrs S.E. Hanks
52 I.A. Wagstaffe

53 Mrs H. Cooper
54 Mrs A.J. Harwood
55 Mrs E. Sears
56 Mrs M.U. Fraser
57 Sue & Tim Ponton
58 B.J. Radbone
59 Mrs E. Chambers
60 Mrs L.G. Eagles
61 Brian Parrott
62 Mrs F.L. Miles
63 Mrs Joan Tacon
64 G.W. Looker
65 Mrs Phyllis Baker
66 Miss Bridget Ransom
67
68 Mrs D.M. Weston
69 Mrs Lucy Scott
70 Mrs C. Mobbs
71 Mrs C. Pugh
72 K.W. Cook
73
74 Mrs S. Cook
75 The Library, West
76 Oxfordshire Technical
    College
77 Mrs Joan Hepworth
78 David & Jean Smith
79 Andrew Logan
80 Mrs R. Partlett
81 J.R. Room
82 Mrs H.F. Embling
83 Mrs M.E. Bedward
84 Mrs P. Scott
85 Mrs Pamela J.M. Hessey
86 Mrs A. Neiland
87 Mrs G. James
88 J.R. Terry
89 Miss Maud Logan
90
91 Doris C. Wright
92 Dr Margaret Noble
93 Mrs J. Sear
94 Mrs I.L. Carter
95 Mrs M. Thomson
96 Mrs Anne Robson
97 Mrs K. Bunce
98 Mrs J.M. McDermott
99 Kathleen Timms
100 Mary Phipps
101 Mrs S. Reavley

102 Mrs M. Cox
103 A.A. Willett
104 Brian Jackson
105 David Jackson
106 Mrs Spivey
107 Jayne Griggs
108 Verdun Dare
109 Mrs P. Zong
110 Brian C. Matthews
111 Mrs K. Page
112 Mrs Mary Winter
113 Ruth E. Kendall
114 Mrs C. Smith
115
117 S.J. Wharton
118 Kenneth & Dorothy
     Smith
119 Stuart Rowles
120 Mrs Eve Gray
121 Mr & Mrs D.J. Noonan
122 Mrs H.M. Hyatt
123 Julia Hiles
124 J. Pollock
125 Mrs B. Carr
126
127 Ian Petty
128 M.L. Johnson
129 Susan Burnell
130 Brian Oscar
131 Henry Box School,
     Witney
132 Edna Mason
133 Norman Lush
134 D.J. Titchener
135 Mrs J. White
136 Diane A. Iverson
137 Mrs Panting
138 Stanley J. Pimm
139 V.A. Brooks
140 Richard Jones
141 Catherine Malcolm
142 D.J. & P.L. Turner
143 G.&R.E. Hayes
144 Mrs P.T. Warner
145 Mrs D.M.M. Robins
146 Madge Woodford
147 Edward Hare
148 Mrs M. Smith
149 Mrs P. Jones
150 L.A. Tacon